The Saturday Book
Thirtieth Year

The Saturday Book

EDITED BY JOHN HADFIELD

30

HUTCHINSON OF LONDON

THE SATURDAY BOOK was founded in 1941 by Leonard Russell and has been edited since 1952 by John Hadfield. This thirtieth annual issue has been made and printed in Great Britain by The Anchor Press Ltd, Tiptree, Essex.

ISBN 0 09 104560 6

The frontispiece reproduces an equestrian portrait by A. F. de Prades of Miss Adeline Horsey de Horsey, who became the second wife of the seventh Earl of Cardigan. (By courtesy of Edmund Brudenell, Esq., of Deene Park.)

Introduction

THE SATURDAY BOOK is concerned with people and things—as distinct from thoughts and theories. In the last two issues we have given a good deal of attention to people. This year the emphasis is on things.

It is an odd fact that in a world where the ephemeral is in the ascendant, and so many things are designed to be expendable, so many people feel a very special need to collect and preserve things that appear to have permanent value. On further thoughts, perhaps it isn't odd: it is cause and effect. Time's winged chariot speeds so fast along the motorways that people long to arrest its passage behind their domestic doors. Hence the increasing rise of prices in the auction rooms and the proliferation of the notice ANTIQUES in the streets of every town and village.

In its time THE SATURDAY BOOK has pioneered a number of collectors' interests, and much of the credit for this is due to our most constant contributors, Olive Cook and Edwin Smith. It is appropriate therefore that they should lead off in this collectors' issue by discussing the art of collecting, and illustrating their theme with examples from their own very idiosyncratic collection. It is appropriate, too, that L. T. C. Rolt, who wrote in our pages about vintage cars and traction engines long before such things became prizes of the sales room, should return with another exercise in mechanical connoisseurship, and that James Laver, our Psychologist of Fashion, should analyse the motives and changes that led up to one of the current crazes, the collection of clothes and the wearing of military uniforms.

And, amongst these engaging examples of the minor arts, it gives us a great deal of pleasure to illustrate some current examples of work by two other regular SATURDAY BOOK contributors who, in their different but related fields of engraving, may well come to be regarded as major artists of our time—Laurence Whistler and George Mackley.

J.H.

Contents

Collectors'
ITEMS

The Art of Collecting

BY OLIVE COOK

PHOTOGRPAHS BY EDWIN SMITH

THE ACTIVITY of collecting is rooted in the origins of human society. It preceded the arts of agriculture and metallurgy, for the earliest economy was based on food-gathering: early man lived by picking and choosing, identifying, sampling and exploring, spurred on by his curiosity and aided by the developing powers of his memory and his ingenuity. The foundations of an acquisitive society were laid long before those of an affluent society; and the importance in the modern world of this oldest manifestation of human culture is revealed not only by the existence of temple-like institutions devoted to the fruits of the collecting instinct but by the fact that nowadays nearly everyone collects, whether it be bronzes or barometers, miniatures or musical boxes, puppets or postcards, coins or carpets, shells or Sheffield plate, books or bus tickets.

Twentieth-century technological man can never return to that golden age when human needs were met merely by searching, comparing and selecting with delightful freedom from the encumbrances, the irksome preparations and the exertion that even hunting entailed. Yet certain forms of collecting stir memories of that elysium, and carry with them a marvellous sense of release and spiritual renewal. It is, above all, the hours spent in looking for natural objects or for discarded artefacts embellished by decay or weather that give exhilarating reality to the dream of effortless superabundance. It is then that collecting can most clearly be perceived to be a creative art in its own right, a true and special expression of personality. For this kind of collecting has nothing to do with fashion or record bids in the sale room: the value of the objects sought or unexpectedly encountered is only to be measured by the degree in which their shape, colour, texture and idiosyncrasies appeal to the visual sensibility and imagination of the finder.

There is one particular object in the modest collection from which the illustrations on the following pages were taken which highlights this aspect of collecting. It is commercially worthless; it is of no interest to the connoisseur, and even the naturalist would scorn it; but the moment when I came upon it lying at my feet in a Yorkshire lane will never be forgotten, so sta .led and entranced was I by this strange, dark, stony form, looking, with its beautiful curling leaf shapes, like some exotic Early English capital. It is a piece of slag from an iron mine.

This lump of dross is among the most prized of a considerable assemblage of found objects. Shells, the most obvious of sea-shore pleasures; pebbles; sea-moulded wood and sea-clouded bottle-glass; fish-shaped rolls of dried mud dashed with coloured shingle; bits of ironmongery, rust-reddened and meta-morphosed by sea action into sculpture; the bleached, fragile skeletons of seabirds; feathers; fossils, mysteriously preserving life in death—these are among the treasures that fill drawers and boxes or impart vitality and diversity to table, mantelpiece and shelf. They are neither catalogued nor classified: they are there simply to be wondered at, to nourish imaginations withered by the over-organised knowledge of our age.

Perhaps the most exciting of these objects are those which are most easily come by—the flints strewing the chalk uplands in their myriads outside my windows. A short walk in winter across the fields of north-west Essex provides opportunities for choos-ing and acquiring which surpass those of the most chock-full junk shop. It is the astonishingly figurative character of so many of the flints which shocks the eye. The forms of a rearing stallion, a crouching hare, a goose, a sleeping swallow, a hand with pointing index, the head of a bull and a giant foot (too big to carry home by hand) were all found on two successive days. In each case chips in the brilliantly white surface of the stones, exposing the jetty core, added a significant detail, the hint of an eye or a nostril just where it was most telling. Even the abundant abstract shapes, rounded and flowing, seem, like the non-figurative sculpture of Henry Moore, who has often spoken of his feeling for flints, to suggest the torsos and limbs of human beings petrified and become one with the landscape.

Ideally, if he is to remain an artist in his pursuit, the principles which determine the collector's choice of found objects should prevail in every field of his activity. But once a collector takes himself seriously he is apt to specialise, and then, developing an extraordinary spirit of tenacity in tracking down the missing pieces in a series or historical sequence of objects, he will seek chiefly for completion, regardless of aesthetic quality. He may even succumb to the desire to be unique in his specialisation, heedless of its subject so long as it is rare, like the Frenchman who owned the one and only collection of *croissants*, acquired from pastry shops and bakers all over the world. Or, regrettably, he may become a curio-hunter, impervious to the ugliness of a piece so long as he is satisfied that it is a peerless curiosity. The summit of his aspirations might then be something in the nature of those famous carvings of Old and New Testament themes executed on cherry or plum stones by the seventeenth-century craftsman Philippe Santa Croce, or the knife made in 1606 by the Austrian Leo Pronner. Only ten centimetres long, it concealed thirteen drawers in its handle, inside which were minute rolls of parchment inscribed with the Psalms in no less than twenty-one languages.

Then again, the collector may all too easily be led by fashion either to acquire something for which he has no passion or to ignore something of outstanding merit. Not so very long ago, in 1939, a writer in a journal devoted to antiques described cottage pottery as 'of common stamp, tawdry colouring and coarse quality', while a popular Yorkshire saying—'like Falsgrave pottery, rough and ugly'—indicated the general estimate of that now highly prized slipware. Only artists and the few independent collectors who were immune to common opinion then had the strength to follow their instincts and to respond to the vigour and variety of Staffordshire figures, to copper-lustre jugs and tea-things painted in daring and unusual colours.

Until recently it was possible in the field of printed ephemera to give full rein to personal taste and sensibility with little reference to market values. The situation has now quite altered. The rise of Pop Art has been accompanied by a veritable craze for collecting postcards, tickets, invitations, trade cards, sale notices, almanacks and every kind of label. Prices have soared, and the mania has produced its own crop of undiscriminating fashion-conscious specialists. There are cheese-label collectors, for example, known as tyrosemiophils and cigar-label collectors called vitophilists.

Even if a collector has the courage and the taste to base his collecting only on personal preferences, rejecting the advice of those who are believed to be good judges, not caring a fig for the argument that such and such an object was once part of a celebrated collection, he may yet fall a victim to certain deplorable vices which are undoubtedly encouraged by his activities. These vices include hoarding, niggardliness, secrecy and avarice. The sixteenth-century collection of Prince Ferdinand of Tyrol in the castle of Ambras, for instance, was less an expression of personal taste than of the Prince's inability to exclude or to discard anything that was brought to his notice. He heaped up his vast accumulations of objects in eighteen great cupboards, where they were found after his death. In addition to his famous collection of weapons he owned four thousand books which were piled in confusion alongside fantastic animal tusks, sharks' teeth, rhinoceros horns, shells, stones, ostrich eggs, lumps of crystal, some of which were adorned with enamelled or engraved landscapes, skulls and skeletons, musical instruments, masks and fans made of feathers, the length of rope with which Judas hanged himself, a magic stag's antler, which, if placed against the wall of a Jew's house on Good Friday, would bleed, pieces of coral, mandrake roots, objects made from human skin, the portrait of a hermaphrodite, stuffed birds, snakes and crocodiles, coins, rare and common, a bronze by Giovanni da Bologna, Ferdinand's contemporary, and the renowned Cellini salt cellar, now in the Kunsthistorisches Museum, Vienna.

The niggardly collector, whose life is centred in his possessions, has been immortalised in the character of Cousin Pons, and La Bruyère describes men who refused to give their daughters a dowry and condemned them to a life of acute wretchedness ('they were hardly clothed and scarcely fed') all on account of a 'lumber room, cluttered up with curios and precious statues, already grimy with dust and dirt, and whose sale would put them all in the clear if only their owners could bring themselves to such an action'.

As for secrecy, the auctioneer Maurice Rheims writes of a great numismatist of our own day who successfully concealed his passion and his collection from his wife until the day of his death, pretending that he was only attracted by trifling odds and ends in the antique shops he haunted. A heavy portfolio volume in his library camouflaged a box containing a unique collection of Greek and Roman coins, valued at more than three hundred million francs. The association of collecting with an atmosphere of intrigue is confirmed by the testimony of Montherlant, an avowed and ardent collector: 'I lower my eyes when I walk past an antique shop,' he writes, 'like a seminarian passing a night-club.'

Avarice is the worst of these vices, for it can turn the collector into a delinquent. The collection of the proconsul Verres, the most dazzling of Roman times, consisted to such an extent of purloined objects that Cicero claimed damages of more than one million sesterces for Verres's robberies in Sicily alone. Even a pope, Paul V, resorted to theft in order to add to his collection the Raphael now in the Borghese Gallery, taking it by force from the chapel of St Francis in Perugia for which it had been painted. And Queen Christina of Sweden was so notorious for her covetousness and lack of scruple that Mazarin, who had himself acquired Correggio's *Sposalizio* by dishonest means, insisted that she should be kept out of his apartments in the Louvre when she visited Paris. 'In case she should ask to see them,' he wrote to his secretary, 'I beg you to ensure that this madwoman keeps away from my cabinets, because otherwise some of my miniatures might get taken.'

It is perhaps only collectors as humble as the author of the present essay, collectors who have never connected their pleasure in objects with the idea of their monetary value, who set little store by rarities or complete sets, who may hope to avoid the most flagrant moral disadvantages of their passion. Yet who among collectors can be entirely exonerated from the weakness of hoarding? A list of our own acquisitions would reveal an assemblage quite as heterogenous as that of Prince Ferdinand,

and only a proportion of it plays a truly active part in the creation of the ambience most congenial to us. And we have certainly not resisted the temptation to specialise in one or two
minor spheres. In each case it was one of the chief joys of collecting, the accidental introduction to a fascinating subject, which
prompted the specialisation.

The sight of a number of traditional British matchbox labels,
framed and hanging in the bathroom of Tirzah Ravilous's house
in Essex, kindled an interest which has resulted in what must be
one of the largest collections of such labels in existence. And,
alas, because specialisation has inevitably fostered the urge for
completion, it includes some examples which, considered individually, are aesthetically worthless. The subjects in the frame
embraced such vigorous woodcuts as the bull and the chequered
border, printed in red, the tiger medallions on their ochre
background, and Captain Webb poised in a vermilion arch
above a sapphire sea, which still enliven some of Bryant and
May's matchboxes. There were also a stag's head on an orange
ground, a pink and indigo Mr Punch, a scarlet and black pistol
with the word *pistol* in riveting Doric lettering, a printing press,
velvety black on clearest yellow, and a pale blue miniature of
St John's Bridge, Cambridge. This range of bold images, all
miraculously adapted to the same small area, was instantly
captivating.

Exploration of the immense field thus opened yielded unforeseen riches. The finest of all matchbox labels proved to be those
made in the Far East for the English-speaking world. All the
cosmic themes of Indian Buddhism, scores of ingenious variants
of the lotus design, exquisite studies of birds and wild animals,
named in English, often with quaint misspellings, and a splendidly virile series of hands, clasped hands, hands holding birds,
hands reaching for stars, hands wielding hammers or flat-irons,
hands clutching daggers, hands tossing dice, wonderfully distinguish the labels of Indian manufacture. But it was those produced in Japan before the beginning of the present century
which most excited us. These miniature woodcuts, made by
anonymous artists, preserve and continue the magnificent tradition of the great Japanese print-makers of the eighteenth

century. Their subjects are those of Kiyonaga, Shunso, Sharaku, Utamaro, Ikyo and Buncho, portraits of courtesans and actors, theatrical scenes, motifs from everyday life, aspects of national festivals, illustrations of legendary events, and studies of animals, birds and flowers, both naturalistic and fabulous, to which have been added charming little compositions inspired by English nursery rhymes in which the figures wear Japanese dress.

Another chance encounter led to the acquisition of a unique collection of lantern slides. A few days after purchasing, for the sake of its amusing shape and gleaming brasswork, a mid-Victorian magic lantern, we were strolling through the Bermondsey market when we spied on one of the poorest stalls, amid a heap of tattered, grimy, cast-off clothing, half a dozen lantern slides, priced at sixpence each. They were unlike any Victorian slides we had ever seen, for they showed photographic figures placed against a contrived background, partly drawn, partly photographed. The simple compositions were perfectly balanced and the slides were very sensitively coloured by hand, the six of them combining to form a short narrative sequence illustrating *Mother's Last Prayer*.

The stall owner, a man as unusual as his wares, a refugee poet with long auburn curls and piercing black eyes, dressed in rags as flimsy as those he presented for sale, announced that these were but specimens of a huge collection of similar slides. He kept them in his room at Camberwell, which proved to be half full of the magic glasses. There were so many that it would have taken weeks to examine them. After a half-hearted attempt to discriminate we became the owners of the lot. The collection of more than three thousand slides, consisting of sequences of from half a dozen to as many as sixty glasses, had belonged to a shoemaker of Kettering, who until about 1920 had loaned them for the regular magic lantern entertainments which, sponsored by the Church Mission Society, the Religious Tract Society, the Church of England Temperance Society, the Band of Hope and similar groups, had formerly played the part of the cinema in the social life of the poorer classes.

As images these slides make a far stronger impact than the earlier drawn and painted glasses; and indeed in their inventive combination of photography and painting, in their extraordinary colour range and their striking use of superimposed pictures, they represent a new mode of vision of far greater interest than that of the academic painting of the period. The stories pictured by the slides are all highly moral in tone: they treat of drunkenness and depravity and the consolations of right living. When we acquired them the sets were in wild disorder and only a few of them were accompanied by texts, the 'lantern readings' which would facilitate the task of identifying the subjects. Gradually, over a long period, we sorted them and tracked down their literary sources. They turned out to be based on the work of popular writers who were moved to focus attention on the sufferings of the poor and to offer them the comforts of religion and, if they had succumbed to temptation, the hope of redemption and regeneration. Prominent among these writers were Mrs O. F. Walton, Amy Le Feuvre, Mercy Stratton, Fanny Eden and, above all, George R. Sims. A comparison of the thin, flat, insipid products of these authors with the pictures projected on to the screen emphasises the originality of the slide-makers, for so intensely felt and so powerful is the imagery that the poor material has been transformed into an unforgettable record of the age.

The pioneer in the creation of these slides, we discovered, was Joseph Bamforth of Holmfirth in Yorkshire, who used local villagers as his models. Joseph's son Edwin used the negatives from which the slides were made to produce postcards. This was the origin of the Bamforth verse cards which aesthetically are certainly among the most exciting postcards ever printed. Enthusiasm for the glasses naturally led to an interest in the cards, and so we now possess a comprehensive collection of verse cards which we have striven to complete even though this means including Edwin Bamforth's earliest productions in which the image is in black and white and the text takes up more room than the picture.

This brief account of our collection of matchbox labels and of Bamforth slides and Bamforth postcards modestly illustrates the way in which the collector's pursuit can enlarge his knowledge in unexpected directions. Another example of this fortuitous concomitant of collecting is represented by the embossed funeral cards shown on page 30. We were attracted by the brilliant technical skill and delicacy of Happy Septima's funeral card, dated 1870, and perceived the same high quality and possibly the same hand in the very different design of the Wellington memorial card. Prolonged scrutiny did indeed disclose that they were the work of one and the same person, who had signed both cards. His name was Wood, and the picture of Wellington's funeral car bore his initials, J.T. This discovery was the prelude to the formation of a small collection of embossed work by this remarkable artist, who signed everything he did. He appears to have been active between the years 1851 and 1875, the date of the card commemorating Jane Eliza Paul. Most of the funeral designs are in the Gothic mode, though one, dated 1865, exhibits the style of late eighteenth- and early nineteenth-century sepulchral art. It shows a sarcophagus surmounted by a draped urn and flanked by weeping willows and mourning females, with an extinguished torch lying in the foreground on a bed of minutely executed roses, forget-me-nots and ivy. But while one of the figures wears classical drapery, the other is dressed in the height of fashion for the mid 'sixties, every detail of her costume meticulously rendered. The microscopic flowery ground is typical of Wood's essays in the classical manner he usually favoured for valentines, in the creation of which he seems to have been as prolific as he was outstanding. These enchanting designs, in which the principal motifs consist of cupids and doves entwined in undulating borders of honeysuckle, forget-me-nots, bluebells, arabesques and swags of roses, set against patterns of incredibly fine lacework, bear a marked resemblance to the plaster decoration of the previous century. One of the valentines almost exactly repeats in miniature the theme of the ravishing ceiling of the saloon at Honington.

An interest in the juvenile drama produced surprises of a different kind. As a boy my husband had haunted Mr Pollock's shop in Hoxton Street, and the old man had given him some of the copper plates from which the earliest toy theatre sheets were made. Many years later we decided to take some prints from them. It was only then that we noticed an etching on the back of one of the plates. It showed two spirited attempts at rendering a horse about to throw its rider. The etching was signed, and the artist was Rowlandson. Another of these plates exhibited a number of characters from a play originally published by Green and reissued by Skelt and entitled *Dred*. These characters included a villain called Dr Jekyll. In view of Robert Louis Stevenson's passion for the Toy Theatre and his addiction in particular to what he called 'Skeltery', is it not likely that this was the source of the fairly unusual name of his hero?

Most serious collectors of works of art, even if they do not buy for investment, occasionally indulge in the dream of a fantastic appreciation in values. And one of the incidental gratifications of collecting is to discover that an object acquired solely for its intrinsic merit and its immediate appeal is at the same time a bargain. The early Victorian sculptures shown on pages 22 and 23 are both associated with this subsidiary satisfaction. The delightful little girl clasping her doll stood unregarded and grey with dust in a dingy shop in York. After passing the window several times in the course of a week we began to be aware of the ingenuity of the composition, of the way in which the realism of the figure was combined with a geometric, exquisitely balanced pattern based on triangles. But it was not until the marble was installed in our home that we looked for the artist's signature. He was Angelo Bienaimée, an Italian who studied under Thorwaldsen before coming to London in about 1828. He was the author of the 'Recumbent Bacchante' at Powerscourt in Ireland, of 'Love Triumphant', shown at the Great Exhibition of 1851, and of many portrait statues and busts, the best known of which is that of Sir Robert Peel at Felbrigg Hall, Norfolk. Several of Bienaimée's pieces were sold in London a year or two ago for more than one hundred times the sum we paid for the statue of the little girl.

The marble bust illustrated on page 22 was found in a yard littered with the spoils of demolished mansions and public buildings: columns, doorcases, mantelpieces, grates, sheets of marble and alabaster, sculptures, ornaments, wrought-iron gates and railings, garden statues, and stone seats. This carving was even more disfigured by stains and dust than the Bienaimée, but the nobility of the conception and the marvellous quality of the material shone through the grime. The work proved to be of the finest grained snow-white Carrara marble and it was set (with a spigot, so that it could be turned) on a pedestal of mulberry and dark green marble skeined with white, selected and moulded by the artist. Again it was signed, though the name had either been overlooked or had meant nothing to the vendor. The bust was by Hiram Powers, the American sculptor of the most popular piece in the Great Exhibition of 1851, 'The Greek Slave', now in the Corcoran Gallery, Washington. The same model sat for this bust, which may have been a study for the head and shoulders of 'The Greek Slave', for the pose is identical. It is an altogether finer work than the full-length figure, for it avoids the weakness of the clumsily modelled hands and the coyness of the attitude.

Enough has been said to indicate that the pleasures of collecting are of another order from those of the antiquary or research worker. Collecting, like any other art, is a projection of personality. Like other arts it is indiscreet, for it bears witness to the collector's indecisions, to lapses of sensibility, when perhaps novelty is mistaken for originality, to the dulling of his love for a particular object and also to the glow of feeling that sweeps all before it. To the true collector a taste for his art becomes his ruling passion and the hours spent in its cultivation are the most delicious of his life. It is one of the most effective of all bulwarks against the outrages of mankind and events, for like love, as Fuseli said, 'it excludes all competition and absorbs the man'.

Opposite, top right: a selection of nineteenth-century matchbox labels made in Japan for export. These miniature prints carry on the fine tradition of the eighteenth-century Japanese woodcut. Centre: a series of four verse cards, 'Don't go down the mine, Dad', typical of the cards based on hand-coloured photographs published by Edwin Bamforth of Holmfirth, Yorkshire, who used the negatives from which his father's, Joseph Bamforth's, lantern slides had been made. Below: a selection of cards embroidered in silk in France during the first world war for sale to the English troops.

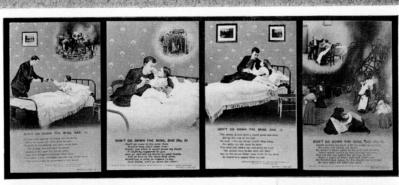

The Victorian figures shown here represent the last flowering of the popular art of the pottery chimney ornament, which began with the eighteenth-century salt-glazed images of stylised Pew groups and horsemen. Though factory-made, these figures are extraordinarily robust in spirit and varied in subject. They were produced by

anonymous craftsmen from two-piece moulds: a whole remove in technique and feeling from porcelain. With their vivid blues and gleaming blacks they are related to the Juvenile Theatre, fairground horses and pictures painted by amateurs on the back of glass like that shown below.

The persistence of the classical ideal is shown by the resemblance of the profile of the Edwardian beauty on the postcard *(left)* to that of the early Victorian marble bust by Hiram Powers. The bust is a study for the American sculptor's 'Greek Slave', the most popular work in the Great Exhibition of 1851. Opposite is a portrait sculpture by Angelo Bienaimée, pupil of Thorwaldsen.

22

Above: glass cases enclosing birds or flowers and fruit of wax or wool were typical Victorian decorations. Below: Bamforth lantern slides combining painting and photography.

Above: The Secret Garden, a German nineteenth-century miniature group. Below: a Victorian leather binding blocked in gold from hand-cut brass blocks.

Opposite, top: Corn dolly made by M. Lambeth, a more complicated version of the cock (chosen for its religious connotations) which traditionally decorated the thatched haystack. Below: Cock, terracotta relief by Bernard Meadows, 1955. Above: Fetish figure from Zanzibar; and left: Italian votive picture, both modern. These objects illustrate the irresistible attraction of symbolism and magic for craftsmen and collectors.

Above: a Forester, one of
three Coade stone parapet
figures, c. 1815. Top, right:
a sheet of characters from
the Toy Theatre play, *Dred*,
published by J. K. Green
in 1855. Right: a lump of
dross from an iron mine.
Opposite, top: a water-
colour by the unknown
painter, Charles Garth,
1806. Below: woodcarving
of St Agatha, c. 1700, and
28 cast-iron doorstop, c. 1810.

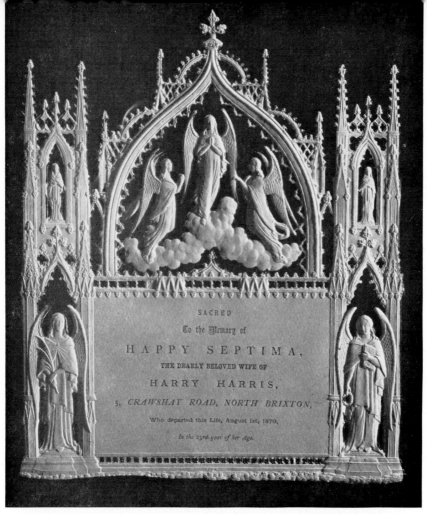

SACRED

To the Memory of

HAPPY SEPTIMA,

THE DEARLY BELOVED WIFE OF

HARRY HARRIS,

5, *CRAWSHAY ROAD, NORTH BRIXTON,*

Who departed this Life, August 1st, 1870,

In the 23rd year of her Age.

WELLINGTON'S FUNERAL CAR

Above: angel and beadwork from a French cemetery. Right: square-base Staffordshire figure with funerary urn, early nineteenth-century. Below: postcard, *c.* 1900. The embossed frame in which the picture is set is a debased version of the splendidly precise and delicate embossed work of J. T. Wood, represented by the funeral cards of Wellington and of Happy Septima Harris (1870), shown opposite.

The Lord's Prayer.

And lead us not into temptation, But deliver us from evil.

Left: Victorian flower container and a collection of Victorian tiles, all transfer printed. Above: sand bell, the decoration carried out in the coloured sands of Alum Bay, Isle of Wight, by W. Carpenter. Below: souvenir plate, made in Ireland.

Top left: Victorian scraps inside a salt-filled bottle. Above: beadwork pincushion and Victorian stuffed regimental hearts decorated with beadwork and tinsel, specially made as souvenirs for soldiers' sweethearts. Below: Victorian shell souvenir.

34

Metal objects. Above: a lead head of Queen Victoria as Empress of India. Opposite, top left: a Sicilian puppet with armour of stamped and beaten tin. Below, left: flower container in the form of a brass and copper boot and stockinged leg. Top right: a Venetian bunch of grapes, copper, 1964. Centre: bronze by Eduardo Paolozzi, 1963. Bottom: brass-decorated iron money box made from a lock, c. 1875.

he woman of a thousand summers back
, wife to that grim earl, who ruled
n Coventry: for when he laid a tax
pon his town, she told him of their tears,

e answered, Ride you naked thro' the town
nd I repeal it

hen rode she forth, clothed on with chastity.

hen rode she back, clothed on with chastity.

then she gained
er bower; whence reissuing robed & crowned
o meet her Lord, she took the tax away,
nd built herself an everlasting name.

Stevengraphs

AND OTHER COVENTRY RIBBONS

BY MICHAEL DARBY

O N THE TENTH of February, 1860, Mr Gladstone announced details of the Cobden Treaty in the House of Commons, one clause of which provided that the duty was to be taken off imported ribbons. This caused a general panic in Coventry, which had been the seat of the English ribbon industry for two centuries, and had for most of that time enjoyed protection from the better designed and manufactured continental productions. Within a few months thousands of weavers were put out of work. While Gladstone certainly acted discourteously in not first consulting the Coventry manufacturers, it could also be argued that the Treaty only completed a process which had begun in 1846 when the protective duties had been reduced to the 1860 level.

Forced to abandon the weaving of dress and furnishing ribbons for which there was no longer a market, many manufacturers turned their looms to the production of woven pictures and bookmarkers. The Jacquard loom used for weaving patterned ribbons was particularly well suited to the production of these ornate silks, and had been employed in Lyons since its invention in 1801 for the manufacture of black and white portraits. James Hart and John Caldicott had both experimented along similar lines in Coventry before the 1860 collapse, the former producing what was probably the first Jacquard woven picture to be made in the town in 1855. Entitled the 'Alliance' ribbon it depicted Victoria and Napoleon III surrounded by flowers and the English and French flags, and was made specially for the Paris exhibition of the same year. Hart's production could hardly be said to be representative of Coventry ribbons in general, it had been produced, like so many of the objects shown at these large

The Godiva Ribbon, woven by J. C. Ratcliff
for the International Exhibition of 1862.
(Herbert Art Gallery and Museum, Coventry)

exhibitions, for prestige purposes alone. Caldicott's portrait of Coventry's Member of Parliament, Edward Ellice, on the other hand, was made in 1858 purely for commercial reasons. He advertised the picture on the front page of the *Coventry Herald and Observer* and exhibited it at Ralph Smythe's, the local art gallery, where it attracted large numbers of visitors.

Caldicott and Hart were among the few ribbon masters who were able to weather the 1860 disaster. Thomas Stevens, the brothers John and Joseph Cash, the old established firm of Dalton and Barton, John Ratliff, and several others, all survived too. Of these Thomas Stevens and the Cashs are perhaps the best known, the former for his large production of pictures called Stevengraphs and the latter for their woven name tapes.

Stevens had set up business in his house in Queen Street in 1854, where for the first few years he experimented with the Jacquard, producing patterned ribbons for a living. The knowledge of the loom's function which he gained during these years enabled him after 1860 to adapt it to the production of more lucrative book-markers. The first intimation we have of this change is a paragraph in the *Coventry Herald and Observer* on May 16, 1862: 'Mr Thomas Stevens ribbon manufacturer of Queen Street has presented sets of his beautifully illuminated bookmarkers to the churches of Holy Trinity and St Michaels.' Stevens must have had several looms at work by this time since it would have been very uneconomical to change the warps in one loom every time that a new pattern was required. This theory is substantiated by his registry at the Patent Office on May 30 of nine different designs for bookmarkers, including examples depicting Shakespeare, Bunyan, and Wesley, and others bearing ecclesiastical sentiments and symbols which were intended for prayer books and bibles. The *Art Journal* called them 'a new branch of art manufacture'; *The Bookseller*, rather unusually at a loss for words, described them as 'register ribbons'; and the *Coventry Standard* hailed 'a new branch of art that gives additional employment where new employment is much needed'.

Success assured, Stevens registered the designs of new examples in June, July, October and November of 1862, amongst which were ribbons entitled 'Thy Bridal Day', 'Thanksgiving',

'Unchangeing Love', and 'I wish you a merry Christmas'.

Besides the production of bookmarkers he also wove several much larger ribbons at this time. One issued in August, 1862, was described in the local press as 'a new and more ambitious effort in portrait weaving by Mr Stevens, the piece being intended as a memento of the Nonconformist Bicentenary; not at all adapted to be used as a bookmark but rather to be framed and hung in the drawing room where its merits as a picture entitle it to the place of honour'. This ribbon depicted Baxter, Owen, Charnock and Howe surrounded by an architectural framework obviously inspired by Pugin's Gothic revival. This style was also chosen by the ribbon's designer Jessie Lee for a similar picture commemorating the Oxford Martyrs, Cranmer, Ridley and Latimer, which came out in September, 1862. These pictures, which are among the most interesting of all Stevens's productions not only for their early date of manufacture but also because they were consciously designed in the contemporary idiom, ill deserve their present lowly position in the estimation of collectors.

With the exception of one other picture depicting the Prince Consort surrounded by his daughters, Stevens produced no more ribbons of this type for another sixteen years, concentrating instead on the rapidly expanding bookmarker trade. He shared this market initially with several other manufacturers. John Caldicott, continuing his earlier trend, registered several designs in 1862 at the Patent Office. It is interesting to note that Caldicott's first registration of a bookmarker depicting Christ and the cross was made on February 18, over one month before Stevens's first registration. Caldicott and Stevens are not the only contestants in the race to produce the first bookmarker. Mr Aaron Lester, a warehouseman in the employ of John Cleophas Ratliff, claimed during a piracy of designs case in the courtroom on October 24, 1862, that 'Our firm produced the first bookmarkers at the beginning of this year, I believe I draughted the specimens produced in January last'. Some future research may help to solve the problem of precisely who did make the first bookmarkers, but what is clear is that Stevens did not have their production entirely to himself during this early period, as has been assumed by many collectors.

The death of the Prince Consort on December 14, 1861, and the International Exhibition of 1862 provided the incentive for a rash of lettered and pictorial ribbons besides bookmarkers. John and Joseph Cash, whose business had been founded in 1846, brought out two ribbons to commemorate Albert's death. One appeared in March, 1862, and was described in the *Coventry Herald and Observer*: 'Certainly the best ribbon of this class we have yet seen is this portrait, not so much for the likeness of the Prince which seems not to have been taken from one of the best originals, but for its accessories of Rosenau, the birthplace of Prince Albert, and of Windsor where he died, which are exquisitely done, each making a pretty little picture as if it were in the best style of engraving.' This ribbon was designed by Thomas Clack, a pupil of the local school of design who later went on to become a principal at the Royal College of Art. Cash's other portrait appeared in June and depicted the Prince, with the Exhibition buildings of 1851 and 1862.

Dalton and Barton, whose business was described by their manager William Andrewes in 1863 as the most progressive in Coventry, also produced two portraits of Albert. One was inscribed 'His Royal Highness the Late Prince Consort' and depicted Albert full face, while the other was inscribed 'Albert the Good' and showed him in profile in an oval medallion with Gothic ornament above, and, below, the royal coat-of-arms. A profile of Queen Victoria in a similar framing was woven at about the same time, and undoubtedly formed a pair with this portrait.

John Cleophas Ratliff produced what was probably the most outstanding ribbon of 1862. Called the Godiva ribbon, it was specially made for the 1862 exhibition. It consisted of a passage from Tennyson's poem 'Godiva' with suitable embellishments designed by Richard Rivington Holmes, then Keeper of Manuscripts at the British Museum. Holmes later became the Queen's Librarian at Windsor and received a knighthood before his death in 1911. The ribbon gained for its producer a gold medal at the exhibition and the commendation of the jury, who stated that 'the more closely it is examined the greater is the astonishment that such a multitude of exquisitely finished details could be produced in such a small space'.

The year 1863 saw the marriage of the Prince and Princess of Wales, and Coventry Town Council decided that they should honour the occasion by drawing up an address of congratulation to the royal couple. At their meeting on March 10, 1863, Alderman Lynes stated that it had been suggested to him that 'the address be woven on a broad Coventry ribbon loom'. It was decided to implement this suggestion and a production committee was set up with the Mayor at its head. The methods used by the committee to select a design for the address caused great dissatisfaction in the town and evoked considerable criticism from the other members of the Council. A Mr Cowsell, manager of the Corn Exchange, was declared the winner of a competition for designs advertised in the local press, but his winning entry was never used. The reason for this was that Ratliff unexpectedly placed at the committee's disposal the loom on which he had woven the Godiva ribbon, thus considerably cutting their expected costs. Ratliff must also have mentioned that he could probably obtain the services of Holmes to design the address too. It is hardly surprising that the Council should have jumped at this opportunity, since Holmes's ability as a draughtsman had been proved, and his knowledge of illuminated manuscripts was beyond question. When completed, the address, which is perhaps the most remarkable of all Coventry ribbons, was presented to the Prince and Princess in October, 1863, in a casket 'enriched with lobed crystals, amethysts, carbuncles and ivory', specially made for it in Coventry by Skidmore's Art Manufactures Company.

Besides this particularly handsome ribbon many favours were produced by a number of manufacturers designed to be worn during the wedding festivities. Similarly, in the following year, which marked the tercentenary of Shakespeare's birth, many favours were woven to commemorate the event. Stevens himself produced three or four different bookmarkers portraying Shakespeare and his birthplace, and adapted the designs for a rosette which was intended to be worn on the day. The three ribbons forming this rosette often become detached from the silk-covered button bearing Coventry's arms which held them together, and have been mistaken for separate bookmarkers.

After the initial rush to produce pictures many manufacturers either went out of business or settled to the weaving of fancy trimmings and elastic goods, leaving the field clear for Stevens to make bookmarkers unhindered. His trade continued to expand, and by the late 1880's he could claim to manufacture more than nine hundred different varieties. For a short while during the 1870's he experienced some competition from the firms of E. Bollans and Welch and Lenton, who had manufacturies at Leamington and Coventry respectively, but neither of whom appear to have been very successful.

In 1875 Stevens constructed an entirely new factory in Cox Street. As originally built it consisted of a basement and two upper floors, each 182 feet long and 40 feet wide, with boiler and engine houses at the rear. It was designed on the most hygienic and economic principles, with a large dining room for the staff and adequate lighting and ventilation. When surveyed in 1901 the factory was described as still catering for the welfare of the employees better than any other premises in the town. The title 'Stevengraph Works' appeared along the front façade, and Stevens specifically refers at this time to Stevengraphs or 'pure silk woven illuminated bookmarkers'. The term Stevengraph nowadays has become synonymous with the silk pictures which Stevens sold in cardboard mounts.

The first picture of this type depicted a stage-coach and horses and was registered at the Patent Office on May 12, 1879. This is the earliest date known in connection with any of these cardboard-mounted pictures. Stevens obviously made the registration with the Yorkshire Fine Art and Industrial Exhibition of 1879 in mind, because here he exhibited a loom, and sold souvenir pictures of this stage-coach with 'London and York' appropriately emblazoned on its door. It is interesting to note that the identical coach and four had been registered as a bookmark in 1872, seven years earlier.

Stevens also sold two other pictures at the exhibition, one depicting Dick Turpin's ride to York on Black Bess, which was registered on May 28, 1879, and the other depicting the first train to run from Stockton to Darlington; this was not registered, but appeared in bookmark form several years earlier. These three pictures proved enormously popular and sold in large quantities for more than forty years.

Joseph Gutteridge, a ribbon weaver who worked for Stevens, has left an account of his life in a charming autobiography entitled *Lights and Shadows in the Life of an Artisan*. He records operating a loom for Stevens at an exhibition in the North of England.

The day after I arrived the loom came and I had a most difficult time owing to the dearth of assistance to get it together but after it was started there was no lack of visitors who wondered that such a strange piece of mechanism could weave eleven different colours of silk into a bouquet of flowers, and form letters on the fabric as though they were printed. Oftimes the number of people around the loom was so great that I had to stop it working or the barriers that protected it would have been broken down. Next to the loom was a stall well stocked with Mr Stevens manufactures.

The Press was full of enthusiasm for the new mounted cardboard pictures and a flood of similar items followed those made at York. 'The Last Lap', depicting a penny-farthing bicycle race, 'Full Cry', depicting a hunting scene, 'The Start', depicting horseracing, and 'The First Point', showing coursing, were all registered in 1879. These were followed in 1880 by further pictures showing the start of the Oxford and Cambridge boat race, Grace Darling, more hunting scenes, a fire engine, and a picture of the Lady Godiva procession, an annual event in Coventry. Within a decade or so hundreds of different pictures were being made, and the manufacture of new bookmarkers had almost ceased. The majority of these framed pictures bear Stevens advertisements pasted on the backs. These, like an earlier series of advertisements which he inserted in *The Bookseller*, often provide a very good clue to dating. The fewer the number of medals and other pictures listed, the earlier the mount. Queen Victoria is listed as the late Queen Victoria after 1901, and mounts bearing the title *Thomas Stevens Limited* date from after 1908, when the firm became a limited company.

Just as Bollans and Welch and Lenton copied Stevens's bookmarks, so W. H. Grant copied the mounted pictures. William Henry Grant had started business in a single room in Foleshill, Stevens's birthplace, in 1882, and expanded his trade so rapidly that by 1884 he was able to exhibit a loom at the Wolverhampton and Staffordshire Fine Art and Industrial Exhibition, where he was selling 'Framed pictures and portraits of distinguished statesmen'. Many of Grant's productions are so like those of Stevens that without inscriptions on the mounts it would be impossible to identify them with any degree of certainty. Grant's exhibit at Wolverhampton in 1884 was followed by participation in exhibitions at Edinburgh in 1886, London in 1890, and Chicago in 1893. On each occasion Stevens also sent a loom. While Chicago was almost certainly Grant's first exhibition in America, this was by no means the case for Stevens, who had sent looms to Philadelphia in 1876 and Cincinnati in 1888.

In 1878 Stevens had moved to Stoke Newington to manage the London end of his ever-expanding business. Never too robust in health, in September, 1888, he underwent an operation on his throat. Complications set in, and he died on October 24, 1888. Thomas Inger Stevens and Henry Stevens, two of his three sons, inherited the business, which continued to produce woven pictures until 1940, when German bombs reduced the Cox Street factory to a pile of rubble. What was left was taken over by the Leek firm of Brough, Nicholson and Hall, and until recently the name Stevens was mentioned in their letter-head.

Stevens was not the only firm to suffer during the blitz; several others were also put out of business. With the closing of Franklins some years ago J. and J. Cash are now the only ribbon weaving firm left in Coventry, and it is gratifying to note that they still continue the old traditions by producing lettered and pictorial ribbons on special occasions.

Until comparatively recently 'Stevengraphs' could be bought very cheaply, but with the recent resurgence of interest in Victorian popular art some of the rarer subjects such as 'Leda and the Swan' and pictures of Newcastle and Blackpool sell for hundreds of pounds. Indeed, Coventry ribbons, and particularly those of Thomas Stevens, have become so popular among collectors that one London auction house holds regular sales exclusively devoted to them, and a Stevengraph Collectors Association has been formed, with its headquarters in New York and members all over the world.

Almost certainly produced for the American market by Stevens in the 1880's

The Home Stretch.

This design was registered on October 31, 1879

The Last Lap.

A design woven by Stevens for the American market in the 1880's

The First Innings.

WOVEN IN SILK BY THOMAS STEVENS, INVENTOR AND MANUFACTURER, COVENTRY AND LONDON. (REGISTERED.)

Are You Ready?

The start of the Oxford and Cambridge Boat Race: registered January 10, 1880. Another picture depicting the finish of the race was made later.

WOVEN IN SILK BY THOMAS STEVENS, INVENTOR AND MANUFACTURER, COVENTRY AND LONDON. (REGISTERED.)

The First Touch.

Depicting a game of Rugby football: first produced in the 'eighties.

WOVEN IN SILK BY THOMAS STEVENS, INVENTOR AND MANUFACTURER, COVENTRY AND LONDON. (REGISTERED.)

The Start.

One of a series of racing scenes. This design was registered on December 15, 1879.

46

A woven
picture of
the Prince
Consort,
showing
the
Exhibition
buildings
of 1851 and
1862.
Made by
J. & J. Cash
in 1863.

LANDING OF COLUMBUS
OCTOBER 12TH 1492.

First made at the Chicago Exhibition of 1893 where Stevens exhibited a loom

The Present Time.
60 MILES AN HOUR.

Adapted from the design for a bookmarker first produced in the early 'seventies

William, Prince of Orange
CROSSING THE BOYNE.

Probably made during the 'nineties

48

Down on the Farm

BY L. T. C. ROLT

WITH DRAWINGS BY LESLIE THOMPSON

FIFTEEN YEARS ago I wrote for THE SATURDAY BOOK a lament on the passing of steam from the farm which ended with a question: 'Is it too much to hope that we may soon see a parade of traction engines, restored to their former glory, snorting proudly round the show ring?' Such is the perennial fascination of steam that what was then only a pious hope has now become a reality. Farm traction and portable engines are now highly prized collectors' items. Barns and farm-yards in Britain have been so thoroughly combed for them that there cannot now be many surviving examples left that have not been hauled out of rusting retirement and lovingly restored to their former glory by a prodigious expenditure of time and money. As carefully groomed as shire horses by their proud owners, they now show their paces before large and appreciative audiences at agricultural shows and traction engine rallies all over the country. One of the happiest features of this movement is that so many of its devotees are farmers. Some have restored their own old engines and given them an occasional useful job to do in addition to taking them to local rallies or shows.

Moving with slow and majestic deliberation, sucking up water from pond or ditch through the long proboscis of its armoured hose, the farm steam engine was an endearing monster. But, like the monsters of prehistory, it was doomed to extinction by its sheer bulk and weight. In some countries where the land was light and the rainfall low, direct haulage of agricultural implements by steam might be practicable, but in England, for most of the year, such a thing was quite out of the question. Here, the steam traction engine had to be restricted to the headlands, hauling plough or cultivator to and fro across the field by steel cables. Even so, when the land was particularly wet and heavy it was difficult to get such a cable ploughing engine on to the field at all. Even the humble farm 'portable' engine, used to provide power for chaff-cutters and other barn machinery, needed a team of horses to move it from place to place. So it was that when the smaller, lighter and more nimble internal combustion engine appeared on the agricultural scene steam rapidly disappeared from the farm. The law of the survival of the fittest operates far more swiftly and ruthlessly in the mechanical than in the natural world.

Nearly forty years ago I worked successively for two small firms of agricultural engineers in Berkshire and Wiltshire. The sale and repair of farm tractors of makes now rarely seen, such as Rushton, International, Massey-Harris, Case, and, of course, the early model Fordson, formed a substantial part of their business. Your farmer has ever been a shrewd and hard bargainer, and the sale of a new tractor could only be clinched by offering him a generous allowance for his old one. This was often a weird and wonderful contraption that looked like a steam traction engine minus its boiler. I once had the job of collecting one of these primitive machines from a remote farm high on the Wiltshire Downs. To start it up and drive it home would have been a far too uncertain and tedious operation, so we decided to tow it away behind a rubber-tyred tractor. I had the job of steering the veteran, and I shall remember that ride as long as I live. It was just as well that there was much less traffic on those Wiltshire byways then than there is today. For the old tractor had steering of traction engine type, with chains controlling a swivelling front axle, and the most frenzied and incessant wheel-winding on my part could not prevent it weaving drunkenly from side to side of the road. My seat was hard, the tractor unsprung, the wheels were shod with steel strakes, and the road was rough. This combination produced a vibration so intense and appalling that I was reduced to a quivering jelly while the machine shed intimate bits of itself as it went along. Because my towing driver could not hear my urgent calls to stop, some of these parts were never retrieved. For all I know they may be lurking in roadside ditches to this day, to be discovered and puzzled over by future industrial archaeologists. I had thought that this was the last primitive tractor of this kind I should ever see; but a few years ago I discovered I was wrong.

Forty years ago, mains electricity had not penetrated far into rural England and the farmer relied on many small engines, not only to drive his barn machinery but to pump his water supplies and generate current. While some of these were diesel engines of fairly modern type, many more were very old and primitive, as I can testify, for, in response to urgent SOS calls from the farmers concerned, it used to be my job, when they broke down, to go out and coax them into reluctant life again. Many of them were of American origin and were called 'Three Mule Team', 'Five Mule Team' and so on according to their power, presumably for the benefit of farming pioneers in the Middle Western States. These were small horizontal engines, looking like small steam engines in that most of their vital parts were exposed to view—and, incidentally, to the dust, chaff and pig-meal which adhered readily to their oily surfaces. Like the farm tractors of those days, they started on petrol but, when they were hot, would accept with reluctance the cheaper paraffin. Their speed was crudely regulated by what was then referred to as a 'hit-and-miss' governor which operated on the principle of switching off the ignition whenever the engine threatened to run too fast.

An American 'primitive': a 1913 Avery 40–80, with flat opposed engine, which slid backwards and forwards to change gear.

An engine so regulated emitted a characteristic coughing and wheezing noise; the heavier its burden the more frequent the coughs, and *vice versa*. For three decades this was a familiar sound on the farm, but now, like an old tune, it can be heard only in memory. Such engines were often cooled by an open tank or 'hopper' of rusty water directly above the cylinder. The recurrent paroxysms produced by the hit-and-miss mode of operation caused the water in this steaming cauldron to slop over, occasionally finding its way into places where water was never intended to be, such as the carburettor or the magneto.

Occasionally engines of this kind displayed spectacular foibles. I remember one such at a lonely house on the Wiltshire downs. It was an unusually large engine and it drove an antique dynamo which would now be considered a prize piece by an industrial museum. It exhausted into a large underground expansion chamber outside the building. Inflammable vapour used gradually to build up in this chamber until there was a violent explosion followed by a miniature earthquake. This happened regularly. Every three months or so we would receive an agitated telephone call and, crying 'It's done it again!', pile into our old service van to repair the damage.

Having served my apprenticeship on steam traction engines and steam locomotives, I had steam in my veins and was inclined to be contemptuous of all 'stink machines', be they tractors or stationary engines. But that was the time of the great Depression when a young engineer was glad to get a job of any kind. Had I been told then that the steam traction engine would one day be lovingly preserved I should have been mildly surprised. But if anyone had assured me that the despised 'stink machines' which had usurped the place of steam would also, in their turn, become collectors' items I should have regarded such a possibility with frank incredulity. Yet this is precisely what has come about.

Collectors are apt to be curiously intolerant of each other. Thus the philatelist is apt to regard the philumenist with patronising amusement as a harmless crank, although to an unprejudiced outsider it appears as logical to collect matchbox tops as postage stamps. Similarly, your steam devotee should pause before he dismisses the collection of early farm tractors and farm machinery of equivalent date as an eccentric pastime. The primitive farm tractor may appear a crude, puny and altogether contemptible machine beside the massive steam traction engine. Yet this is a case of David and Goliath, for in the light of farming history the tractor is by far the more significant machine.

The effect of steam power on agriculture was limited. Too expensive for the small farmer to afford, the majority of owners of steam traction engines were steam ploughing and threshing contractors. It was in the large, flat fields of the great corn-growing districts of East Anglia that steam came into its own. In the hillier lands of the north and west steam power was employed to a much lesser extent, and in some areas it was almost non-existent. Steam brought about no significant decline in the population of farm horses. Indeed, it relied on horses to some extent. A set of steam ploughing tackle at work, for example, needed horses to draw its supplies of coal and water. The first primitive tractors, on the other hand, represented the spearhead of a farming revolution that has now eliminated the draught horse altogether.

Although the evolution of machines is a much more rapid process than the evolution of natural species, there is, none the less, the same 'inevitability of gradualness' about it. The first specimens of a new mechanical species always betray a close family resemblance to the species they are about to supersede. They lose these vestigial traces either by a slow process of adaptation or when some engineer of particular genius and foresight re-designs them from the ground up. So, just as the first motorcars resembled horse carriages without the horse, the first farm tractors, when they were born in America, resembled steam traction engines without the boiler. They were even called 'Gasoline Traction Engines' and their design was simple and crude. A large single- or twin-cylinder horizontal engine, running at slow speed and with a heavy flywheel, was mounted in a simple frame in place of the traction engine's boiler. This engine drove the rear wheels through a cone clutch and large, exposed gear wheels. The first of these ungainly, coughing monsters (they were the very devil to start) was actually a converted steam traction engine, built in Chicago in 1889. Primitive though it was, it was lighter than the original traction engine and it needed no coal or water, which was quite a consideration in the Middle West of America. Its success was such that a number of different makes of 'Gasoline Traction Engines' were built in America over the next twenty years or so. Some of these, notably the 'Waterloo Boy', the 'Titan', and the 'Overtime', were exported to England, and it was on one of these that I made my ever-memorable

The 'Waterloo Boy', 1917, model 'N', 12–25, made by the Waterloo Gasoline Engine Company, of Waterloo, Iowa.

journey in Wiltshire. Some early tractors of the same primitive type were built in England; but only one of these, the Saunderson, succeeded in competing seriously with the American machines.

It is a sad fact that the reason why Britain lost her proud position as the workshop of the world was not a lack of engineering initiative but a strange failure on the part of the commercial world to recognise engineering genius and give it adequate backing. The history of the farm tractor illustrates this point very well. For the first man to realise that the American type of tractor was merely an unwieldy compromise and that to take

full advantage of the new power on the land he must forget the
steam traction engine and design a completely new form of
tractor was an Englishman, Daniel Albone. His tractor was
called the Ivel, and it was first built at Bedford in 1903.

It is significant that although I had so much to do with farm
machinery at one time I had not, until a few years ago, heard of
Daniel Albone and his Ivel tractor. I assumed, as I suppose most
people do, that the prototype of our modern farm tractor was
the American Fordson, which was first imported into Britain
in 1917 as part of the effort to counter the effect of the U-boat
blockade. Then, a few years ago, I saw one of the three surviving
Ivel tractors in the hands of a private collector and realised that
in this small, neat and compact machine Albone had come up
with the right answer fourteen years before Ford. This proves the
value of collecting. No catalogue engraving, no faded photograph could have enabled me to appreciate the genius of Daniel
Albone as did the sight of his actual creation.

The Ivel tractor was acclaimed by agricultural engineers on
both sides of the Atlantic; but Albone died in 1906 and with his
death British initiative failed and it was left to the Americans to
follow where he had led. It is true that the Americans had the
advantage of a very large home market which enabled them to
produce their machines in great quantity. Nevertheless, it seems
extraordinary, after such a brilliant start, that all attempts to
make a good British farm tractor during the years between the
wars failed miserably, with the result that our fields were almost
entirely populated by American machines. One of the most
ambitious of native efforts, the Rushton tractor, was almost a
carbon copy of a Fordson, and failed only in those few features
in which it departed from the American original. The engineer
who was ultimately responsible for putting an end to this sorry
state of affairs was Harry Ferguson of the Ferguson tractor, the
originator of the tractor-mounted implement.

Today there are in Britain two main collections of 'post-steam'
farm machinery, both on farms and made by enthusiastic
farmer-collectors, one in Northumberland and the other near
Ross in Herefordshire. I have not so far had the good fortune to
visit the former, which specialises in early stationary engines, but

it was on a visit to the latter that I saw the Ivel. It was a nostalgic day for me, for the Ivel was only one of many. There were not only examples of early 'Gasoline Traction Engines', looking as improbable as those fanciful machines dreamed up by Heath Robinson; there was an example of that dismal failure, the Rushton, miraculously surviving; and there were specimens of those American machines which had once lorded it in English fields, tractors with which I was once so familiar but never thought to see again. Agricultural machinery since the passing of steam is a neglected subject and such ardent collectors and restorers deserve the greatest credit. For their work enables us and future generations to understand what life was like down on the farm forty or fifty years ago.

Acknowledgements are made to Charles L. Cawood, Esq., of Grimthorpe Manor, Pocklington, York, for supplying historical material and help with the illustrations.

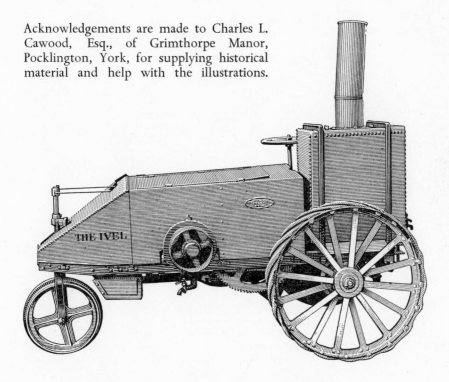

The 'Ivel', the original show tractor of 1903

Poster by 'Pal'

Early Transport Posters

BY D. B. TUBBS

'APLAGUE on this Klimt who dresses up our *bicyclettistes* in trappings from Byzantium and the early Frankish tribes', cried the Paris dressmakers when Sarah Bernhardt returned from Vienna with a trunkload of outlandish costumes. They had good reason, for what the divine Sarah wore upon the stage soon found its way on to the hoardings, and to be Frank was at one time the cycling girl's ambition. Paris during the Belle Époque was a city of posters, and it would not be too much to say that its gaiety was the creation of one man, the artist and lithographer Jules Chéret, one of the pioneers of the art of the lithographic poster. When Chéret set up shop in 1866, with backing from the parfumier Rimmel, the new Paris of Baron Haussmann was thought by many to be a pretty drab place; the old medieval buildings and narrow streets had been swept away, to be replaced by uniform avenues of chilly façades in a neo-Mansard style, built by the mile and as yet unrelieved by trees. The drab 'new town' aspect of Paris was bedecked by Chéret with gay posters advertising not only theatres, ballets, music halls and student dances, but shops, cosmetics, lamp-oil and cough-drops.

J. L. Forain may have sneered at *ce Watteau à vapeur*, but Chéret was indeed the last fling of the French rococo, and his girls the very essence of gaiety. So popular were they that Chéret was invested with the Légion d'Honneur 'for creating a new branch of art, by applying art to commercial and industrial printing'. One of his very last poster designs, drawn in 1900 before he abandoned posters for painting, was an advertisement for petrol—Benzo-Moteur, Essence Speciale pour Automobiles, to be had in sealed and capsuled cans.

Chéret was by no means alone amongst artists of mark in working for the new transport industries. J. L. Forain made an elegant drawing for the second Salon du Cycle, a great improvement upon the poster (by E. Clouet), showing *poilus* pedalling away from their bivouac towards *La Gloire*, a realistic drawing in the style of the illustrated papers and dated 1892. A realistic treatment was used also by the anonymous artist of a slightly earlier era to advertise a strange tricycle by the Howe Machine Company Ltd of Glasgow, an agonisingly complex affair with large wheels behind and a small one in front. This firm, like most British cycle-makers during the boom of the 'eighties and 'nineties, maintained agencies in Paris; and one French constructor, Bouglé, proprietor of Cycles Michäel, even adopted an English name and manners. This 'L. B. Spoke' was a friend of Toulouse-Lautrec, who met him at the Buffalo velodrome and drew two posters, for Cycles Michäel, and La Chaîne Simpson, for which 'Spoke' was the French agent. Neither drawing succeeds, because Lautrec's eye, so infallible for human and equine anatomy, was not at home with chains and sprockets. It is one of the tragedies of advertising history that Lautrec drew no motor-car posters. That they would have been splendid is shown by his portrait of Tapié de Celeyran, his cousin, in motoring cap and *peau de bique*. Certain it is that Lautrec knew many of the fashionable ladies—and demi-mondaines—who used to enliven the Bois de Boulogne, first with their cycling costumes, then with De Dion motor tricycles, and finally driving out in the new-fangled horseless carriage, collateral descendants of the 'pretty horsebreakers' whose spanking pony phaetons had stopped the traffic in Hyde Park some twenty years before.

Paris was fortunate in having the Bois; it was the nearness of the Bois which made Paris the world headquarters of motoring. Not only was it the fashionable rendezvous, but also a splendid testing-ground for the French motor industry, most of whose factories lay in the industrial suburbs adjoining the Bois to the south, north and east—Levallois, Boulogne-Billancourt and Bois Colombes. Aristocrat and artisan could meet upon each other's doorstep, a happy arrangement exemplified by the partnership of Comte Albert de Dion and the ingenious mechanic Georges Bouton. Cycling and motoring in France, therefore, were essentially urban, metropolitan pursuits, not distributed throughout

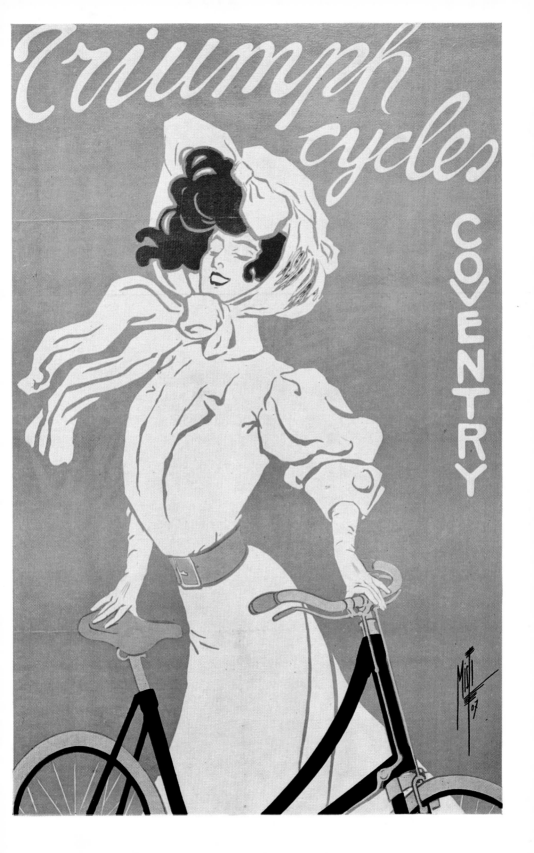

a nation of sportsmen as in England; and artists of every school lived close at hand. Most of the big names worked for the cycle or motor industries at one time or another. The poster-collector will find every *fin de siècle* style represented, from the urban realism of Steinlen to the highest rarefications of *Art Nouveau.*

Théophile Steinlen (1869–1923) came from Lausanne but identified himself with the Parisian scene. Moving outside it for a moment he drew a striking poster for Motocycles Comiot, a boldly outlined figure of a motor-cycling girl in red blouse and boater forcing her way through a flock of geese *(left)*; he also made a poster for De Dion, showing one of the cars *full size,* but with little of interest apart from the format.

On the whole De Dion publicity, although voluminous, was not very inspired. The cars, being exceptionally easy to drive, were aimed for a feminine market. Most of the posters show cars being driven by women, usually accompanied by a uniformed chauffeur or Negro 'motor boy'. One such poster, with two cars, is signed by the artist 'Misti', and one feels that he was under orders not to make his girls too attractive for fear of offending the clientele; but Misti could draw pretty girls well enough, for while working for Triumph cycles he produced a most striking Gibson Girl type, boldly presented in the style of of the Beggarstaffs—James Pryde and William Nicholson (see page 61.) His hand is also to be seen in an unsigned poster for Hurtu cycles—a name which sounds less frightening in French than in English. The central figure is a Gibson Girl, very bold and be-bloomered in black with leg o' mutton sleeves, wasp waist and boater against a plain yellow background (see page 68).

We have said that styles varied. Nothing could be more different from the boldness just described than the posters put out by the Automobile Club de France for the Salon in 1902 and 1903. The Belgian artist, Privat Livemont, was almost as well known as that great name in *Art Nouveau,* Sarah Bernhardt's friend Alphonse Mucha. Like Mucha, Livemont has a passion for rare plants cunningly arranged to embellish his allegories. He too introduces fancy lettering to form part of the design, but where Mucha is jewelled, he is muted, with the pale, subtle colours which in France led to *Art Nouveau* being described as *le style Liberty.* For 1902 the heroine is a remote blonde goddess *(right),* seated in a flower-strewn De Dion (the Comte, later Marquis, was on the committee) dressed in a muslin gown and bedecked with Wagnerian trappings; she is shown in a cone

of light from an overhead lamp, against a nocturnal view of the Grand Palais. Technical details abound: steering and control levers, brass lamps, street light complete with arc burners, a cycle wheel and an arrangement of games equipment, for this was the *Salon de l'Automobile, du Cycle et des Sports.* The same dilute autumnal palette, the same blend of allegory and technical realism, may be seen in French banknotes to this day, proving that *Art Nouveau,* despite the current revival, has never really died.

Contemporary with Steinlen and Privat Livemont was Eugène Grasset, a medievalist and 'post-Pre-Raphaelite'. Once again muted greens and browns, and the cool, impersonal girl. He made a beautiful poster for Georges Richard, manufacturer of cycles and cars, whose trademark was a four-leafed clover. This emblem forms the central theme of the poster, held by a girl—or goddess—whose other hand rests a trifle incongruously on the handlebars of a bicycle. The directors of Georges Richard had every reason to be proud of their poster, but some of them may have seen it as a triumph of art over engineering, and one feels that F. Ramsdell's beautiful design (page 64) may have found an equally mixed reception in the boardroom of American Crescent Cycles at Chicago, for an improbable wind is blowing the damsel's hair and draperies so as to obscure the mechanical details. Here again a leash of greyhounds would appear more appropriate, but as an example of *Art Nouveau* display work with affinities to William Morris, Burne-Jones, Mucha and the *style nouille*, it could hardly be bettered.

'Pal', otherwise Jean de Paléologue, worked for both French and British manufacturers, and his pretty model is to be found in many posters, realistic and allegorical. British firms leaned towards realism. Almost audible are sturdy Midland voices enjoining 'Pal' to 'let customers see the bicycle', and to include a man in the picture. Thus for Whitworth Cycles *(right)* 'Pal' has a handsome fellow in full cycling kit—cap, loose jacket, knickerbockers, knee boots, with U.V.F.* lapel badge—supporting a cycle, all its lines and mechanism clear, with one finger beneath the crossbar to demonstrate lightness and balance, admired by Pal's model and two of her sisters wearing Mrs Bloomer's brainwave, while three more pretty girls peer down on them from a wall. For Humbers the catchword again is speed: the model *(right)* in waspwaisted *tailleur* and leg o' mutton sleeves alone in the country with her swain, having left her companions behind. 'When you ride a Humber, my dear,' says he, smugly lighting a cigarette, 'you always have to wait for the

* Union Vélocipédique Française

68

others.' The Humber people were rather strong on masculine appeal. Another of their posters shows a smartly attired, very British sportsman descending the steps of an hotel, while a page-boy in buttons stands holding his cycle (page 58). *Très* snob, *prèsque* cad.

This Norfolk-suited realism superseded the allegorical manner of the mid-'nineties, when Paléologue was in business as the Atelier Pal, 44 rue St-Lazare, Paris. From tentative beginnings, in which his model, this time swathed in operatic fancy dress, a palm in one hand, a four-leaved clover in the other, poses beside photographs of a Georges Richard cycle and horseless carriage, he moves on to the full treatment. Symbolically provided with hammer and anvil, his faithful model poses, completely topless this time, above a landscape showing the factory of Adolphe Clement, '*La plus vaste usine du monde*'. A similar approach was used by E. Vavasseur for Peugeot—a Junoesque woman, elbow resting upon a globe, receives the homage of an aproned workman with bicycle, one of his hands indicating the works of *Les Fils de Peugeot Frères* lying below in a valley, in the rays of the rising sun. Similarly Raymond Tournon for Cycles Brilliant; here the background is a bird's-eye view of Paris, while a partially draped lady, seated upon yet another symbolic anvil, holds in the same hand a palm-frond and a bicycle. The appeal of such posters must have been limited—which would explain their short life-span. There is a certain perverse eroticism about the best of 'Pal'. His model for Clément is definitely 'topless', not classically bare-bosomed, and there is a similar illicit thrill built into an S.C.O. poster, in which a topless lady clearly intends to go cycling, holding cycle and palm-frond, her dress caught by a single ribbon, legs cross-gartered to the knee (see page 63.) Kinky, one might say; and how different from the frolics of Chéret, whose motto was '*Toujours les femmes et les rires*'. By the middle 'nineties the laughter has departed and the women are remote.

During the 'nineties poster-collecting became a cult. Copies of each new poster could be purchased, as they came out, from the print dealers and stall-holders along the Seine, sometimes in both the published form and *avant lettres*—without lettering. Collectors unwilling to pay, or beguiled by the element of risk, preferred to suborn the itinerant fly-poster or strip the newly hung poster from the wall with water and a sponge. Many a Chéret and Lautrec was obtained in this way. Collectors were served by two magazines at least, *The Poster* in London and *Les Maîtres de l'Affiche* in Paris, each of which ran for five or six years; but by 1900 the craze had spent itself; most of the *maîtres* were dead or otherwise engaged, and it was felt by many that decadence had set in, that the future lay not with the artist but with the illustrator.

What of Edwardian motoring art? Touring-car advertisements tend to be dull, mere illustrations, except when the artist has been fired by the excitement of inter-city racing. There were some humorous posters in the style of Cecil Aldin and Lawson Wood (including some French imitators), but the main inspiration came from E. Montaud and his school, which, for purposes of the record, may be said to include Guy Lipscombe, a painter who joined *The Autocar* as art editor in 1907. The monstrous racing cars of the early years made a wonderful subject for posters, which manufacturers of cars and accessories were quick to appreciate. Not only were these thunderous dust-raising vehicles exciting in themselves but dramatic effects could be heightened by drawing attention to the attitudes of passengers and spectators. One of the first to realise this was Noel Dorville, author of a famous poster for Huile Rigal, in which the bearded, gnome-like occupants huddle in the cockpit as their car gathers way, while a hundred yards behind, alongside one of the quais on the Seine, a Paris–Madrid 'Dauphin' Mors makes ready to start (see page 62).

Pierre Simmar, too, pulls out all stops for a poster based on Perrault's tale of Hop o' my Thumb (see page 66), whose companions have commandeered a Peugeot and are racing through a gorge, the car at an impossible angle, silhoutted against a dust-cloud, pursued by the giant in seven-league boots. The dust, the pursuer and the leaning car give great urgency to the composition. In another Peugeot poster, by G. de. Burggraff, a woman in big hat and motoring veil, fur-coated man beside her and headlamps blazing, drives straight at the viewer, while smoke and dust clouds trace the word Peugeot in the sky. There is a hint of SF here, and more than a trace of *Art Nouveau*; but for a

virtual anthology of the latter we may look at the poster
with which Richard-Brasier (successors to Georges Richard)
advertised Théry's Gordon-Bennett victory of 1904 (see page 73).
The car is in profile, the rear half enveloped in dust. Driver and
mechanic sit hunched at the controls, while from the front of the
car emerges horizontally an unearthly allegorical figure typifying
speed, her hair *en nouille* to produce the 'speed lines' which were
one of the early discoveries of the motoring artist, in this instance
Bellery Desfontaines. Touring-car publicity at this time still relied
upon pretty girls and a fashionable image to convey its message;
the racing marques quite rightly made a hero of the car.

The most prolific, most famous and in many ways the best of
Edwardian racing-car artists was E. Montaut, who knew (and
probably invented) most of the tricks for conveying drama and
speed. His principal living came from a lithographic studio for
the production of sporting prints to commemorate cycling,
motor-cycling, automobile and flying events. Montaut's collection entitled *10 Ans de Courses* appeared in 1907, and it would not
have been in nature had manufacturers not sought him out.
During the next seven years some excellent posters appeared
signed by Montaut, and by his pupil, Gamy. They give their
message pictorially, with a minimum of type-setting, and it
would be hard to find any clearer or more charming evocation
of the Belle Époque than, say, Montaut's poster for Renault, in
which a country-house tennis party, having arrived in a Renault
coupé de ville, break off their game as the airship *Le Lévrier* (*moteur*
Renault) flies gracefully over the court.

The *école* Montaut was not always so realistic, however. There
is a Jules Verne flavour about some of their productions. It is a
charming conceit to bring the Grand Palais Vulcan to life, indicating a balloon, airship and aeroplane forming a background
to the first Aeronautical Salon (see page 66); but Montaut and
Gamy could move even further in the direction of SF when encouraged by such clients as Splitdorf Magnetos. In one of these
Gamy has been struck by the likeness of a high-tension magneto
to the bonnet and radiator of a car; his poster shows a car com-
posed mostly of magneto hurtling in Gordon-Bennett fashion
through a gorge. This would seem to be a piece of friendly

plagiarism because some years before Montaut himself had depicted a racing car of normal type braving an electric storm. The summit of each crag is formed by an automobile magneto, the central one issuing forked lightning. Three lines of caption only: a heading *L'Allumage Moderne,* and, below, the words *Magnéto/Lavalette Eisemann.*

Montaut prints have now become rare and expensive. However, visitors to Paris or London feeling in anthological mood should visit the Michelin Tyre depots in the Boulevard Péreire and Fulham Road. Designed by a House architect, François Espinasse (1880–1925), the London depot is one of the purest *Art Nouveau* buildings extant, and its tiles, inside and out (but no longer, alas, some stained-glass windows destroyed by bombing in World War II) are well worth a pilgrimage, for ceramic posters are unusual to say the least. These examples are probably not by Montaut or Gamy; they are more likely to be by Sevelinge or E. Cousyn, who had a greater penchant for the schematic *Art Nouveau* tree and for the flat areas of colour derived by Toulouse-Lautrec from the Japanese print. The Fulham Road depot was built in 1910, but the trademark 'tyre man' still used in Michelin publicity dates back a good six years further, when the company's slogan was *'Le Pneu Michelin boit l'obstacle!'*. An artist named O. Galop painted a man made of tyres crying *'Nunc est bibendum!'* as he raises a goblet filled with nails and broken glass, while *Pneu X* and *Pneu Y,* his neighbours at table, cringe in dismay. An historic poster indeed.

The French school had its imitators. Guy Lipscombe in England, who made some exciting insurance posters, and a number of Italian artists essayed to naturalise the style. An amusing poster for Diatto composes the car itself from the letters of its name, and sets the whole contraption flying through the air, fairy-tale fashion, to the bewilderment of a story-book magician. The Triestino artist, Leopoldo Metlicovitz, bridged the gap between Montaut dramatics and classical allegory by providing a naked Roman god to urge his motor-cars along, an interesting departure from the pretty-girl convention.

American manufacturers and the top end of the French and Italian carriage-trade continued to stress the High Life theme;

nothing could be more aristocratic than a poster for the Padus car, of Padua, who employed the painter Omegna to put this message across.

For sheer light-hearted elegance, however, there has been no one to touch René Vincent. His delicate, calligraphic line and complete sympathy with both mechanism and human beings have never been excelled. He made catalogues for Berliet and for Hispano-Suiza, and at least one beautiful pair of large lithographs for Peugeot. The writer has not yet been lucky enough to see a poster by him; but if the French motor industry failed to commission any, they were neglecting an opportunity. *Je m'en fiche des affiches* would be no motto for a sales manager, especially in the Belle Époque.

The illustrations are from posters in the Montagu Motor Museum at Beaulieu, Hampshire, with the exception of those at the foot of page 62 and at the foot of this page, which are in the collection of James O. Barron, Esq.

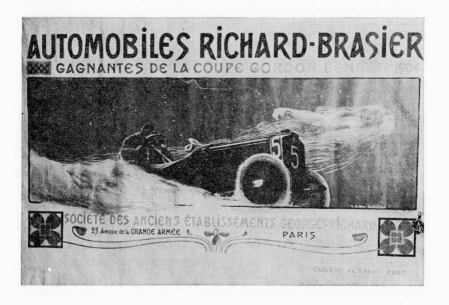

A Glitter of Glass

BY ANNA HADFIELD

Nearly thirty years ago, at one of Knight, Frank and Rutley's auction sales in London, my husband bought for twenty-five shillings two of the tall ale glasses illustrated on page 83, and made me a present of them. He bought them just because he liked the look of them. Those two glasses were a pleasure and an interest to me through the dreary years of war, and were the start of my very small and modest collection of eighteenth-century drinking glasses.

At that time I knew nothing at all about glass, ancient or modern. To me, these glasses seemed unusual and also beautiful, and I did not think that they were modern. My interest and curiosity were aroused. I began to read books about glass, and old English drinking glasses in particular, and to keep my eyes open. I found that there was a great deal to learn, and that a lot of it could only be learned by experience. I also found that, as in many specialist fields, experts are liable to disagree.

After the war it became possible to see and even to handle the kind of glasses I had seen only in photographs. The day when I actually bought one was a day of anxiety and triumph. The time has long since gone when a good glass could be bought quite cheaply in some country antique shop. But it could be then. Today I imagine that almost all the exciting discoveries have been made. Though there are many antique shops, there are less than a dozen dealers with real specialist knowledge, and most good glasses pass through their hands, via Sotheby's and Christie's. The amateur collector, unless he is going to buy his knowledge dearly, would be well advised to stick to these dealers. They will treat him fairly. It is also important for the would-be collector to see and to handle as many genuine glasses as possible. Sotheby's and Christie's have several glass sales each year, and many fine collections pass through their hands. It is always possible to view—and even to handle—the glasses a day or two before the sale.

Although from the mid-seventeenth century to the end of the eighteenth century drinking glasses were made in an astonishing variety of shapes and sizes, proportion is the safest guide to identifying a glass of that period. Some failure of proportion between bowl, stem and foot so very often betrays the fake. It is not important for the amateur to be able to date a glass exactly, but it is important that he should be able to spot a 'wrong-un'.

A Venetian, Giacomo Verzelini, who came to London in 1571, was the first man to manufacture glasses in England that attained the high quality of those hitherto imported from Murano. They are beautiful glasses, richly decorated with diamond-point engraving on bowls that are a smoky-brownish colour. But they are extremely fragile. I believe that there are not more than eight glasses—or parts of glasses—surviving that can be ascribed to Verzelini. If one should come up for sale at this present time the would-be purchaser must be prepared to spend several thousand pounds to get it.

The 'collector's' period of English drinking glasses dates from the late seventeenth century to the beginning of the nineteenth. This does not mean that one should refuse an offer of a sixteenth-century Verzelini goblet as a birthday present, but merely that many glasses have survived from this later period, enabling representative collections to be formed. For this we have to thank George Ravenscroft and his chemical knowledge. In 1673 he built a glass-house in the Savoy, London, and here he started experimenting in an effort to manufacture a 'metal' that was clear, like the soda metal used earlier in the century, but also strong and durable. Sometime between 1674 and 1676 he patented a new metal which contained oxide of lead. Unfortunately many of his early works suffered from a disease of the metal called 'crizzling', which caused the glass to become opaque. But by the time George Ravenscroft died in 1681 he had got the proportions of his mixture absolutely right. This metal—known as glass of lead—had a special richness of texture and tint, and was also strong. It made possible the manufacture of the great variety of glasses that followed, with all their differences of bowl, stem and foot formation.

The first phase following George Ravenscroft's discovery was that of the heavy baluster glasses, an example of which is the large goblet illustrated on the opposite page. This has a round-funnel bowl on a knopped and true baluster stem, with a folded foot. It is nearly nine inches high. Fairly early in the eighteenth century even heavy baluster glasses tended to become smaller. Gradually complicated knopped stems gave way to balustroid stems and plain stems, making the glasses lighter. The Excise Tax, which was levied on glass in 1745, made a necessity of this trend.

The description of the various stem formations, knops and shapes of bowls has given rise to a lot of conflicting expertise. There are drawn-trumpet bowls, bell bowls, thistle bowls, double-ogee bowls, bucket bowls—all of which terms are self-explanatory. There are drop knops, annulated knops, mushroom knops, acorn knops, ball knops: in this context a variety of different terms is used. Although the terminology changes, as new books are published, I still find one of the earliest books, *Old English Drinking Glasses* by Grant R. Francis, 1926, as useful a stand-by as any other book of reference.

Only a novice in the field will be misled by the term 'Kit-Kat glass', which still persists, as a description of a glass with a drawn-trumpet bowl, rising from a ball knop at the lower extremity of its stem. In fact the drinking glasses shown in Kneller's portraits of members of the Kit-Kat Club are quite different—more like the right-hand glass illustrated on page 78.

It is no doubt true that a cheap claret glass does as much justice to the wine as an expensive eighteenth-century goblet. But old glass has an appeal similar to that of old silver—both to touch and to look at it is a joy. Many people may prefer the more 'fancy' glasses—the opaque and colour twists in the stem, the engraved and enamelled bowls. But I prefer the various types of baluster glass. Their beauty is a classical one: it lies in their shape and proportion, and in the light that plays on the rich-textured metal and glitters in the tears in knop and stem.

THE WORD 'baluster' derives from a Greek word meaning the flower of a pomegranate. Architecturally it is a column with a pear-shaped swelling at the lower end. Either true or inverted balusters are combined in the stem formation of many early eighteenth-century glasses and are the chief decorative element in the design of drinking glasses between about 1680 and 1740. The earlier glasses followed hard on the heels of George Ravenscroft's invention of 'glass of lead' in the late 1670's. They are called heavy balusters, as opposed to the lighter balustroid glasses made later, as, for example, in Newcastle. However, the term baluster may be applied to any glass with a heavy, many-knopped stem, even though it may not actually contain either a true or inverted baluster. Of the glasses illustrated above, the handsome glass in the middle is 6⅝ inches high. It has a solid-based bell bowl above a collar knop. The stem consists of a flattened knop above a true baluster stem. The foot is domed and has a wide fold. All these glasses have folded feet: the metal was turned under the edge, thereby strengthening the rim of the foot.

THESE TWO glasses, both 6⅞ inches high, are of an unusual and rather beautiful shape. The stems, which are drawn from the trumpet bowls, have a slight swelling below the bowl, and each stem contains a tear. Each terminates in a ball knop placed just above a domed foot. These are heavy glasses, and very satisfying both to handle and to look at, the metal having a rich and what one could almost call 'oily' texture. Since every eighteenth-century glass was individually made, these two are not absolutely identical. But the unusual shape and the colour of the metal would make it seem obvious that they were made at the same time, in the same glass-house, and probably by the same gaffer. An interesting point for the collector is that although they happened to be bought in the same sale room, they came from different collections, and after the purchase of the first glass more than two years elapsed before the second glass came up for sale. Apart from the domed foot and the unusual swelling in the stem, this type of glass became known early in the eighteenth century, as a Kit-Kat glass.

THESE THREE elegant glasses, with their drawn-trumpet bowls, and their long thin stems terminating in feet with a good high instep to them, are lucky to survive until today. They are toasting glasses, and this type of glass was used from about 1700 to 1740 to drink a toast, usually to a lady, and probably in champagne. The custom was for the drinker to snap the glass between finger and thumb immediately after drinking, throwing it into the fireplace or under the table, to prevent its being used for any lesser toast. The glass in the middle is nine inches high.

THERE WAS little variation in the design of the feet of glasses in the eighteenth century. In the earlier years they could be domed or folded, and sometimes both. Later they became conical. There was more scope for variation in the stem and the bowl. The glass on the right above has what is called 'Wrythen' decoration, and would have been used for strong ale. The glass on the left has an unusual shouldered stem. The central glass above shows a trace of Venetian influence and was probably made in the late seventeenth century. The middle glass below is known as a Silesian-stemmed glass, and is thought to have become popular with the arrival of George I in 1714.

WITH one exception, the glasses illustrated on these two pages have stems containing air-twists or opaque-twists—sometimes called cotton-twists. The popularity of the air-bubble or 'tear', which occurred accidentally, encouraged the gaffers to experiment. They found that an air-bubble could be drawn out into a thin thread running the length of the stem. It was not long before they found that they could develop this into the air-twist proper. At first this was usually in a drawn-trumpet glass, like the two glasses on the right of the left-hand bottom photograph. The middle glass is a little unusual in that a domed foot is seldom found with an air-twist stem, and it is probably a fairly early glass. Air-twist decoration soon developed into the opaque-twist. By drawing out white enamel rods (or 'canes') within the stem elaborate and beautiful results could be achieved, as in the ale glass pictured above on the left, in which two twists are intertwined.

83

THESE two glasses—6½ inches high—with their round funnel bowls and complicated many-knopped stems, are typical of the beautifully proportioned and elegant balustroid glasses made in Newcastle between 1730 and 1780. Designed for toasting the Jacobite cause, these probably date from around 1745, and are engraved with the simplest Jacobite emblem—a seven-petalled rose and one bud.

Strike a Light

BY AMORET
AND CHRISTOPHER SCOTT

YOU CAN, of course, rub two sticks together until they smoulder; and breathe on the glow; and feed it with little pieces of paper; and fan it with your hat. Generations of Boy Scouts have done just that. Most people prefer to extract the glow-worm from the dashboard of the car, or flick the knob of a butane gas lighter; some eccentrics still use matches.

How easy it all is, how painless and dull and clean and straightforward. How marvellous and romantic it would be to turn back the pages of time and to face the problem of producing a flame with the equipment our Georgian forbears used. Here we are then, at six o'clock of a January morning, with the ice three inches thick in the well, the pump frozen solid, and the kitchen range dead. You take your tinder box, and out of it you fetch the flint and steel; and for five or six minutes you hit one against the other, as your knuckles bleed and your nails tear and the scraps of charred rag in the tinder box refuse to smoulder. When at last they do, you catch a flame with a sulphur match and, your mouth full of brimstone from the fumes, light the first lamp. And there you are, all ready to start on the job of clearing out the dead kitchen fire. How marvellous! How romantic!

The man who invented the striking match should have his name flashing from the top of the Post Office Tower and the Empire State Building. Unhappily, what really happened was that John Walker, a Stockton-on-Tees pharmacist, forgot to patent his invention and died almost unnoticed. A lot of other people made money out of his lack of business sense.

But that was some way on in the search for the ideal 'instantaneous light contrivance' (as most of the researchers call it). The eighteenth century gave birth to a succession of the most engaging devices, some of them extremely dangerous, some remarkably sophisticated, and all of them intended to improve the unhappy lot of—not the housewife, as one might imagine; she had a kitchen maid to light her dead fires for her, and who cared about kitchen maids? It was the smoker who called the tune, the smoker who couldn't light his pipe on a windy day.

All the early inventors turned their energies towards standardising and mechanising the flint-and-steel process: for the five or six minutes mentioned earlier is no exaggeration—it was an expert housemaid under ideal conditions who could catch a light in less than three. A great fillip in this direction was the invention early in the sixteenth century of the flint-lock mechanism for firearms. It was not long before mock pistols were being made for smokers, in which pulling the trigger made the flint spring forward against the steel: the spark ignited a train of gunpowder which in turn set fire to a piece of tinder. All this happened inside the pistol barrel, which then sprang open like a mussel-shell and presented a flaming wad to the expectant pipe. Another form of tinder pistol made in the early eighteenth century had almost everything needed for the early-morning comfort of man. You set a clock, and at the required time a bell rang, the flint leaped to the steel, the gunpowder went off, and a lighted candle emerged triumphantly to greet you (and occasionally to set fire to your bed curtains).

Another quite different method of creating a flame was being explored in the eighteenth century. Every schoolboy knows that a magnifying glass focussing the sun's rays will produce enough heat to set a piece of paper on fire. Georgian schoolboys knew this too, and one of them grew up to patent a smoker's portable burning tube. This was in the form of a small pocket folding telescope with the lens at one end only; inside the other end of the tube you put a piece of tinder. By moving one tube up and down inside the other you could focus the sun's rays exactly on the tinder, and as soon as it was smouldering you pushed a sulphur match through a slit in the side. The invention never really caught on, simply because the sun rarely shines in the British Isles.

Most of the inventive talents were concentrated, however, on finding mixtures of chemicals that would produce fire on contact with each other. There are plenty of them, and chemical knowledge was extensive. This was all very well under laboratory conditions, but the competition to produce the first universal, foolproof apparatus was so keen that every inventor who felt he had the answer would bring it on to the market at once. There was a time during the latter part of the eighteenth century when people were walking around with thin glass tubes of vitriol in their pockets, with lumps of red and white phosphorus, or twists of mixed potassium chlorate and sugar—all of them substances that a modern chemist treats with great caution.

Representative of what was going on, in all its simple awfulness, was Mr Hoppie's heavily advertised product of 1766, Thunder Powder. This 'newly-invented phosphorus powder' was specifically designed for lighting pipes. It probably did this very successfully; the difficulty would have been to confine it to the job in hand. The Instantaneous Light Box showed a much more sophisticated application of mechanical principles to chemical potency. The light was achieved merely by pulling a string, but the train of events this started was a complicated one: the glass stopper rose out of a phial of vitriol; one drop fell on to the head of a potassium chlorate match which burst into flame; the match swung round and lit the wick of a spirit lamp; and the next match moved into place. This apparatus, in its japanned metal box, was intended for use by bed-ridden invalids.

Another chemical device was the electro-pneumatic lamp, which worked on the principle that a spark in the path of a stream of hydrogen produces a flame. But what a chance was seized to turn this prosaic piece of knowledge into an apparatus worthy of the finest salons of the land! Ladies and Gentlemen, let us present to you the Temple of Vesta! Note the Corinthian columns, the doorway in the style of the Adam brothers, the mahogany base. Touch the button, Madam, and see the flames shoot out of the golden lion's mouth! And if I could just have a word with you on the quiet, Sir, all you have to do is fill it up inside with Spirits-of-Salt and bits of zinc, and rub its bottom with a bit of fur—static electricity, you understand, Sir.

At the turn of the eighteenth century neo-classicism was in full flow, and the Temple of Vesta (patented 1807) was a typical product of the age. In the same mould, though hardly as heroic, were the Promethean Matches patented by Samuel Jones in 1828. They were about the size of modern matches, but they were actually tiny glass phials of acid, covered in paper impregnated with a potassium chlorate and sugar mixture. You had to carry a pair of pliers; one nip and your Promethean burst into flame.

But the great moment was upon us. Walker's Friction Lights (flat cardboard sticks, tipped at one end with a mixture of potassium chlorate and antimony sulphide) appeared in his pharmacy in 1831, selling at one shilling a hundred, twopence extra for the tin. All you had to do was to grip the head in a piece of sandpaper and pull smartly. With no patent, Walker's invention was plagiarised wholesale as soon as the news spread: Jones' Lucifers, Watts' Chlorate Match, Bell's Lucifers—they were all direct copies of the self-effacing Walker's invention.

Samuel Jones went further, and in 1832 patented the Fuzee. This was a fat cardboard match which would smoulder for a minute or two after being struck on its sandpaper sheet; it was designed exclusively for smokers. So too were Vesuvians, introduced by Palmer of Camberwell in 1849. But where the Fuzee smouldered, the Vesuvian flamed, and flamed with such intensity that no wind could blow it out. It was altogether a monstrous thing, and both the early models had unfortunate defects. They had huge, pear-shaped heads made up of various combustibles held together with gum and tipped with Walker's striking compound, all moulded round the end of a wooden shaft. So fierce was the flame that the shaft invariably burned through before the head had finished flaming, so that the latter probably fell into your waistcoat pocket. The improved model had a glass tube for a stem, to avoid this comet effect, but the result was that the flame now tended to shoot backwards down the tube and singe one's cuff.

Other strange developments for the smoker were Cigar Tips and Cigar Caps, both introduced in about 1845. The instructions for Le Verrier's Newly-Invented Planet Cegarlights read as follows: 'Stick one of the lights into the centre of the end of the Cegar, rub it gently, against the rough part of the box, and begin to smoke as soon as it is lit! It will burn like a coal for five minutes and not cause any unpleasant smell or taste.' This was a

Cigar Tip. Cigar Caps were shaped like coolie hats in pink card-board, to fit round the end of the cigar.

By this time, however, the 'strike anywhere' match was firmly established, and only the dedicated smoker bothered with the complications of such things. Everyone else carried matches, bought in chip-board boxes almost indistinguishable from those we buy today (except for the labels, eagerly collected by what people who aren't matchbox label collectors call philumen-ists). But because the safety match was still in the future, most people preferred to carry their matches in something rather less easily combustible; and there came into being an enormous selection of little containers that are the delight of collectors. Some of the earliest patent boxes actually went to the length of housing each single match in a separate compartment, rather like a miniature honeycomb.

Probably the most recognisable of the Victorian match-con-tainers are the little flat silver or plated boxes that hung on the end of a man's watch-chain. They nearly always have a ribbed striking surface formed in one end, and having been designed for wax matches they are about half as long as a modern matchbox.

Between about 1850 and 1910 the imagination of the makers knew no bounds. Match containers were made in the form of people and animals (pigs were specially popular), arms and legs, shirts and trousers, pianos, crowns, whistles, bottles and jugs, pillar boxes, milk churns—and so on. The only unifying thing about them is that somewhere there are serrations to make a striking surface: it may be quite clear, it may be on a separate plate inside the lid, or it may be cunningly hidden. There are containers in the shape of bears and dogs where the striker is the animal's rough fur. Most of them were in metal, but a very con-siderable quantity of wooden ones were made, incorporating a sandpaper disc as a striker, or occasionally a separately fixed metal plate. Notable too are the ebony and ivory crowns made at the time of the Jubilee in 1887.

Now the search was on for a pocket-sized mechanical lighter. From France came a succession of devices filled with those little explosive packets known as *amorces,* activated variously by pulling, twisting, scratching or rubbing some part of the container.

At this point it would be as well to mention the quite extra-ordinary part that France played in the development of fire-making appliances. Throughout the nineteenth century France produced invention after invention, many of which were immediately taken up in England and re-patented under a new name. Most of the devices we have described first saw the light in a French workshop, and it was only the *amorce*, a sort of percussion cap consisting largely of white phosphorus, that found no favour in England. The French loved them, and used them in strings, rolls, cylinders and every possible combination. The Americans showed interest, and in 1865 the Repeating Light Company of Springfield, Mass., marketed a lighter in the form of a little drum, with a nozzle sticking out of the side and a rotating handle. Turning the handle rubbed an *amorce* on a rough surface inside and a jet of flame shot out of the nozzle. Just the thing for a lady's handbag.

1870 saw a short-lived counter-invention from Germany, a handsome Greek lamp which merely required its two handles to be pressed together to produce a flame at the spout (achieved by a lump of phosphorus-based compound revolving inside against a rough surface).

The steel wheel for striking sparks from a flint arrived (from France) in 1909, the spirit-lamp petrol lighter a year or two before. But for years pocket lighters were regarded in England as not quite nice, and vaguely connected with Gallic untrustworthiness. Describing in 1926 'modern pocket tinder tubes', those flameless, fizzing dangling things that foreigners use to light their indescribable tobacco, the Bryant and May Collection's catalogue says this: 'Among civilised peoples, the use of the Flint-and-Steel Method of fire-making has survived to this day only in the form of certain pocket tinder tubes, which continue to be made and used in France almost exclusively, mainly as a result of the badness and dearness of matches in that country.' Our soldiers, as well as the French, were glad enough of them in the trenches of the Great War, for a flame drew unwelcome attention at night. We still have an aversion to lighting three cigarettes from one match—the third smoker usually got the sniper's bullet.

Pictures on Glass

by Laurence Whistler

A S LONG AGO AS 1950 THE SATURDAY BOOK drew attention to the then little-known art of diamond-point engraving on glass that was being practised by Laurence Whistler, the poet. Indeed, the present fame of Mr Whistler's exquisite work may be said to have originated in that first serious appraisal of it.

Last year Messrs Agnew put on a one-man show of Laurence Whistler's latest work at their gallery in Bond Street, which attracted an astonishing number of viewers and resulted in every exhibit being sold within a fortnight. In 1972 there will be an exhibition of Mr Whistler's work in the United States.

As a further interim report on the development of Mr Whistler's highly individual art and technique we reproduce some recent examples in the following pages. These reflect a view of life which links his glass engraving closely with his prose book, *The Initials in the Heart*, and his poetry, *To Celebrate Her Living*. As he himself explains it, he regards the external world—the particular settings in which a man lives out his life, whether by chance or choice—as the given material into which he infuses his meanings. The external world has its own meanings, independent of man, and since all things were created for good, good they must fundamentally be. In an ideal state the subjective and objective meanings would be in harmony, though capable of the infinitely varied combinations of happiness. But something is wrong: wrong with man certainly; and perhaps wrong with nature; wrong with time and death as he experiences them. Precisely the same surroundings could be infused with joy for one, with terror for another, and with mere boredom or contentment for a third.

In Laurence Whistler's view, though happiness can never be pursued for itself, it is still the purpose of being; but most often the reality is happiness longed-for rather than achieved, lost as soon as found, remembered or foreseen rather than tasted; and this is reflected in the meanings man reads into his surroundings, and the meanings he expresses in the works he makes.

In the illustrations which follow we see how Whistler's view is expressed in small pictures, about $3\frac{1}{2}$ inches high and 6 inches wide, each engraved in reverse on the far side of a glass goblet, so as to invite the eye right into the concave world of the scene, suspended in transparency. But how to persuade an imagined landscape to convey a meaning? That is the problem of this artist. He takes a hint from the kind of effect we often meet in our surroundings and dismiss as accidental. An object, say a wood on a hill or a window in a wall, may appear too simple and too emphatic to be 'natural'. Ambiguities of shape occur. Outlines of hills seem to cross. Things seem to wear expressions, or to point at one another, or consciously to 'rhyme', resembling each other. A simple shape, say that of gables or lines of plough-ing, seems to dominate a scene. Accidental it is, but it appears intended, breaking out from the profusion and mere random-ness of things-as-they-are.

Simplification, emphasis, ambiguity, expression, pointing, repetition, subjection to a form, these are devices used by this artist—together with symbolism, whether unexplained, or con-tributing to obvious allegory. The notes that follow, based on conversations with the artist, may help to elucidate the signifi-cance of his work.

FROM THE DEAD TO THE QUICK *(opposite)*. The trees come round both sides of the bowl so that we seem to be looking into and then out of a circular grove. On the nearer side (hardly seen in the photograph) they are rotted and fungus-grown, with a line of rubbish between them; on the farther side they are in spring-leaf. Beyond, a sunrise-scene contains the same looped symbol of felicity seven times over. But whereas in Egyptian art the *ankh* is extended on the end of a visible sunray, here each one, though pointing to the sun, appears to be accidental, a chance arrangement of twigs or leaves, a hill or a domed building. The meaning: felicity is in the landscape, or in the eye that would discover it there.

FROM THE DEAD TO THE QUICK

EXACT TIME: APPOINTED PLACE. A car waits at twilight beside a country road, with lights extinguished, for a rendezvous. The place is where the line of the road runs up into the spire, and the sides of a shed-gable exactly meet and are extended by two crossing hills. The time is when the new moon just balances on top of the spire. These are like precise co-ordinates: there can be no other place and moment in the world like this. Thus the meaning is uniqueness, or the once-onlyness of experience.

THE ENCOUNTER. Here the meeting is explicit. Two figures approach one another down a gallery with no visible end, which at the same time appears to be a bridge. Urns of flowers mark the seasons. The wall opposite the sunlit windows is blank, but with a plain door.

MOUNT OF OLIVES
(*left*). A figure looks out on
the modern world through
tree-trunks that assume
demonic forms of mockery.
The night sky is full of
signs and wonders. In the
circle of radiance round
the bowl there is an allu-
sion to Henry Vaughan:
'I saw Eternity the other
night, Like a great ring of
pure and endless Light.'
Below is the same glass
seen from the other side.

WET LANE TOWARDS
EVENING (*right*). 'To-
wards' in both senses. Here
the artist comes nearest to
naturalism, but this im-
aginary scene is pinned to
three bright points—the
road, the sea, the valley—
as if it were held in balance,
while the light grows clear
after the rain.

A SENSE OF SUMMER
(*left*). This is both the subject of the picture and the title of the book propped on someone's knees in the foreground, for an awareness of Summer going on outside has dissolved the room. But the frontispiece of that book shows the same scene in miniature—room, figures and book. So an infinite series is postulated: at every stage upwards the room may be a picture in a larger book; at every stage downwards the page portray a smaller room. It is a metaphor for the serial nature of awareness. The couple are aware, aware of being aware, and aware again of that.

THE SIX OF SUMMER
(*left*). Six intervals of sunlight down a shadowy lane that ends in a small hole like a camera's aperture. The name suggests a playing card — the Five of Hearts, the Six of Diamonds. For in the same way that a card is dealt, unforeseen, this moment of awareness has been given —a chance encounter with Summer on an empty road.

THE WISHED FOR. A wrinkled sky towards nightfall over a landscape where forms cross and merge. A shaft of sunlight holds for one moment, as it turns, the floating symbol of all serious wishing.

THE GAY MAUSOLEUM. It stands, beflagged, on a hill-top
with the landscape seeming to extend from it: between the sterile
and the fertile, and answered by the far country beyond them.

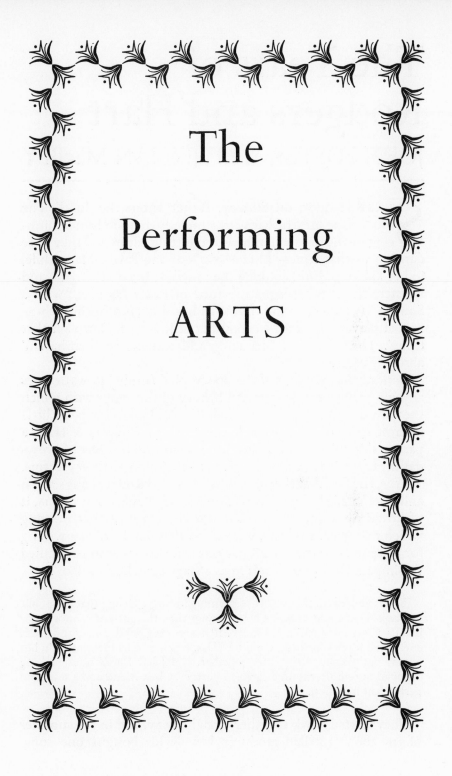

The

Performing

ARTS

The Years of Rodgers and Hart

JOHN FOSTER WHITE & IAN MacBEY

SHARP at noon on Sunday, Father enters the 'local'. The music tape fills the bar with a melody that sets him reminiscing of the days when he was courting Mum and they were dancing to that tune—'Blue Moon'—at the Palais. Meanwhile, in her kitchen Mum, cooking the lunch, turns on the radio and registers the familiar signature tune of *Family Favourites*, 'With a Song in My Heart', as she shouts to her unseen offspring whose record player threatens to spoil her enjoyment, 'Turn off that thing'. The strains of Ella Fitzgerald serenading 'Manhattan' abruptly cease.

None of the members of this apocryphal family knows or cares anything about the origins and history of the songs with which they are simultaneously involved. It would probably be of little interest to them that each is the work of Rodgers & Hart, a partnership whose songs have become so much a part of everyday life that few thoughts are given by the many to their creators.

True, the fact that they met when Richard Rodgers was sixteen and Lorenz Hart twenty-three, one Sunday afternoon in 1918, is of little importance in itself. It was the effect of that meeting which mattered. Rodgers, who up to that day had been writing for pleasure, and the occasional amateur show, has since recalled the impact Hart made on him as a stage-struck schoolboy:

> He was violent on the subject of rhyming in songs, feeling that the public was capable of understanding better things than the current monosyllabic juxtaposition of 'slush' and 'mush'. It made great good sense, and I was enchanted by this little man and his ideas. Neither of us mentioned it, but we evidently knew we'd work together, and I left Hart's house having acquired in one afternoon a career, a partner, a best friend and a source of permanent irritation.

They started work together straight away, and in the summer of 1919 the comedian-producer Lew Fields bought one song,

'Any Old Place with You', for his current Broadway show. In 1920 Fields went further and acquired the entire score of a Columbia varsity show they had written, for his new musical comedy, *Poor Little Ritz Girl*. Although he subsequently replaced some of their songs with others by the more experienced Sigmund Romberg, this may still be reckoned the first professionally staged Rodgers & Hart musical.

After this, however, they were to make little or no public progress for the next five years, apart from one brief return to Broadway in 1924 with *The Melody Man*, a comedy with two songs, written in collaboration with Lew Fields' son, Herbert, under the perhaps significantly uninspired pseudonym of 'Herbert Richard Lorenz'. Ironically, the plot concerned a struggling composer; a theme for a full-scale Rodgers & Hart score, if ever there was one!

The tide turned, in a spectacular and even romantic fashion, in the spring of 1925 when the Theatre Guild put on a fund-raising revue, *The Garrick Gaieties*, for two Sunday performances. Rodgers & Hart provided the songs for a hitherto unknown cast. The show so enchanted audience and critics alike that it was promoted to a regular run that lasted nearly six months.

The song most closely identified with *The Garrick Gaieties* is 'Manhattan'; actually written and then shelved, perforce, some years earlier. This gay yet touching love letter to New York must have struck a refreshing note in the year of such jolly rompings around the hit parade as 'Don't Bring Lulu', but its very originality may account for why it did not fully establish itself with the wider public until a long time later.

In September 1925 Rodgers & Hart underscored this success with *Dearest Enemy*, a wry costume piece; the book by Herbert Fields based upon an incident in the War of Independence. The score introduced the lilting 'Here in My Arms', and the whole show cast a satiric eye over the bosom and buskin operetta as then personified in *The Vagabond King* and a heavily yearning *Student Prince*. Irreverence was to be a never-ending source of inspiration to them both.

If 1925 was the year of breakthrough, then 1926 was the year of consolidation. It began modestly enough with a night-club revue, *The Fifth Avenue Follies*, which doubtless justified the five-dollar 'roll and butter' charges, but left few crumbs in the way of remembered songs. And after that the girls took over, starting with *The Girl Friend*, who now epitomises our over-the-shoulder concept of 'The Gay 'Twenties', ensconced in her perennial 'Blue Room'. This and the title song, along with 'Mountain Greenery' from a second edition of *The Garrick Gaieties*, were later heard in a successful London show, also entitled *The Girl Friend*, but which had no other connection with her American cousin.

Now Rodgers & Hart made their first trip to London, to supply a score for *Lido Lady*, starring Jack Hulbert, Cicely Courtneidge, and Phyllis Dare as the tennis champion heroine. For this they imported 'Here in My Arms', and Hart shot an oblique glance at West End geography to enable Miss Courtneidge to advise Harold French, somewhat inaccurately, that 'A tiny flat near Soho' was 'quite the proper place to go-ho'. Its successful run at the Gaiety had not even begun, however, when Rodgers & Hart sailed back home on the *Majestic* to round off 1926 with two more Broadway shows, which opened on consecutive nights the week after Christmas. *Betsy* was their one flop of the year; a misbegotten miss in search of matrimony, only remembered for the interpolation of Irving Berlin's 'Blue Skies'. *Peggy-Ann* was a very different young lady, a Cinderella-type heroine who wistfully enquired, 'Where's that rainbow?' and indulged herself in a series of Freudian dream sequences. She too came to London played by Dorothy Dickson, but with Herbert Fields' book ponderously anglicised, even the locale being shifted from Glen Falls, N.Y., to Littlenest, Hampshire.

The following month Rodgers & Hart themselves returned to the West End, to see *Lido Lady* and meet C. B. Cochran, who commissioned them to do the score for his 1927 revue, *One Dam Thing After Another*, at the London Pavilion. From this came one of their greatest, most durable songs and the legend that goes with it. 'My Heart Stood Still' is said, *ad nauseam,* to have been inspired by a narrowly avoided accident to a Parisian taxi in which Rodgers & Hart were riding. No reason to doubt it, but if all those who have told the tale as eyewitnesses were actually present, the wonder is that it was not the cab that stood still. Introduced by Jessie Matthews and Richard Dolman, the song also owed something to the then Prince of Wales, who brought it unexpected publicity when one night he instructed the orchestra at the Café de Paris in both its haunting melody and its perfectly balanced lyrics constructed almost entirely of monosyllables.

Rodgers & Hart bought back 'My Heart Stood Still' from Cochran later in the year for their next Broadway production, *A Connecticut Yankee*, based on Mark Twain. Here it shared the honours with 'Thou Swell', a cunningly contrived mingling of mock-medievalism and current slang. The Yankee achieved over four hundred performances in New York, but was no more than a fleeting visitor to Daly's under a slightly changed title two years later.

With their next six shows they marked time, never achieving more than moderate success, and in *Chee-Chee* complete disaster. Only one major Rodgers & Hart ballad belongs to this late 'twenties period: 'With a Song in My Heart'. Written for *Spring is Here* in 1929 and then brought to England for *Cochran's 1930 Revue*, it now seems permanently enshrined as the signature tune of B.B.C. Radio's *Family Favourites* programme. But at least well up in their second division were 'You Took Advantage of Me', sung in *Present Arms* (1928) by Joyce Barbour and a Busby Berkeley not yet the maestro of the flying camera, and 'A Ship Without a Sail' from *Heads Up* (1929).

The 'thirties opened with *Simple Simon*, produced by Ziegfeld, in which a far from simple Ruth Etting reminisced of 'Ten Cents a Dance'. Then it was back again to London, to renew their always happy association with Cochran in *Ever Green*. Opening at the Adelphi in December 1930 it gave Jessie Matthews one of her greatest successes in 'Dancing on the Ceiling'; a song written for *Simple Simon* and unaccountably rejected by Ziegfeld.

With *Ever Green* safely launched, its story of a girl impersonating her own grandmother untroubled by thoughts of the generation gap to come, Rodgers & Hart set off along the fashionable trail to Hollywood where they stayed for five years; only returning to Broadway for *America's Sweetheart* in 1931. This was their last collaboration with Herbert Fields and, ironically enough, a satire on the film industry. The neat topicality of 'I've Got Five Dollars' (shades of *The Fifth Avenue Follies*) as an antidote to the Depression did not deter Dorothy Parker from commenting in *The New Yorker* that Hart's rhymes were 'less internal than colonic'.

The films on which they worked did not add much to the art of the cinema, but *Love me Tonight* produced 'Lover', 'Isn't it Romantic' and 'Mimi' for Jeanette Macdonald and Maurice Chevalier; the last becoming almost as much a part of the Chevalier ambience as 'Louise' and 'Valentine'. Bing Crosby sang 'Easy to Remember' in *Mississippi,* and what began as 'Prayer' for Jean Harlow in the never-released *Hollywood Revue of 1933* re-emerged as 'The Bad in Every Man' for Shirley Ross in *Manhattan Melodrama,* and finally struck gold on its own as 'Blue Moon', the only major Rodgers & Hart song unattributed to a stage or screen production.

1935 saw them back on Broadway with a scintillating score for Billy Rose's mammoth circus-type musical, *Jumbo,* that included: 'My Romance', 'Little Girl Blue' and the exhilarating fast waltz, 'The Most Beautiful Girl in the World'. Then in 1936 they advanced on the world of ballet with *On Your Toes,* and for the first time participated in writing the book. Perhaps the most completely melodic of all their scores, *On Your Toes* is incandescent with numbers of the calibre of 'There's a Small Hotel', the sprightly title song, and 'Quiet Night'. But what undoubtedly gives it an extra dimension is Rodgers' gangster ballet, 'Slaughter on Tenth Avenue', a work which has in its own right achieved the status of a minor orchestral classic. Sadly, however, in England *On Your Toes* proved to be, in the words of yet another of its songs, 'Too good for the average man'.

Babes in Arms in 1937 was entirely their own thing, including the book, and reflects their never-ending empathy with show business. Youthful in theme and casting alike, it has left the biggest single legacy of lastingly popular songs to be found in any Rodgers & Hart score: 'Where or When', 'The Lady is a Tramp', 'Johnny One Note' and 'My Funny Valentine'. And even these may not obscure the wit and charm of its less well-known numbers, such as 'Imagine' and 'You Are So Fair' with its ingenious use of every meaning and spelling of the word 'fair'; still less Hart's splendidly cynical observation in the lyric of 'I Wish I Were in Love Again':

> The furtive sigh, the blackened eye,
> The words 'I'll love you till the day I die',
> The self-deception that believes the lie.

I'd Rather Be Right was almost a diversion, for which they produced a score so closely allied to the theme of George Kaufman and Moss Hart's satire on the Roosevelt Administration that none of its songs retain independent popularity except 'Have You Met Miss Jones?' which Bobby Howes later introduced to London in a wartime revue called *All Clear*. George M. Cohan returned to Broadway to play the President in *I'd Rather Be Right*, and his own big number, 'Off the Record', fortunately remains on the record as re-created by James Cagney in Cohan's screen biography, *Yankee Doodle Dandy*.

Possibly a trifle battered by their encounter with the doughty but difficult George M., Rodgers & Hart kept to themselves again in *I Married An Angel*; a title and synopsis in one. Its best-known song, 'Spring is Here', emphasises the increasingly disenchanted undertow of many of Hart's love lyrics; but there is an infectious rippling gaiety to 'I'll Tell the Man in the Street' and 'Did You Ever Get Stung?', the latter re-written by other hands as 'Little Workaday World' for a film version in which Nelson Eddy and Jeanette Macdonald concluded their own partnership.

An adaptation by George Abbot of Shakespeare's *A Comedy of Errors* now inspired them to more distinctive purpose in *The Boys from Syracuse;* bright as a penny in 'This Can't be Love' and 'Sing for your Supper'; richly mellifluous in 'Falling in Love with Love' which contains the couplet commonly cited as the example *par excellence* of Hart's brilliant flair for internal rhyming:

> Caring too much is such a juvenile fancy.
> Learning to trust is just for children in school.

Although *The Boys from Syracuse* did not come to London until 1963, 'Falling in Love' was sung with great charm by Binnie Hale, wearing a wimple, in the 1940 revue *Up and Doing*.

After victory at Ephesus Rodgers & Hart rather rested on their laurel wreaths with *Too Many Girls* and *Higher and Higher*. At least we owe to these scores the plaintive cadences and introspective thoughts of 'I Didn't Know What Time it Was' and 'It Never Entered my Mind'; and, more esoterically, 'I Like to Recognise the Tune', which took a sly dig at the big bands of the day that all too frequently hid the harmonies in harmonics. Viewed as a whole, however, both these musicals lacked the questing spirit that imbues all the best of Rodgers & Hart's later work.

The case was altered, the situation redeemed, in 1940 when they found in *Pal Joey* the makings of their masterpiece. Out of John O'Hara's imaginary letters of a seedy Chicago night-club entertainer, and all-round opportunist, they created the exuberant score of the most adult and wholly integrated musical comedy yet put before an audience. Taking a cue from its most celebrated number, it was a show that at first, and variously, 'Bewitched, Bothered and Bewildered' everyone who saw it. 'Can you draw sweet water from a foul well?' somewhat sententiously enquired the distinguished critic Brooks Atkinson, confronted with the witty audacities of 'Take Him' and 'In Our Little Den of Iniquity'. Time has proved you can. *Pal Joey* had a respectable enough original run but a decade later it was revived on Broadway to outrun any other Rodgers & Hart musical. *Pal Joey* finally reached London in 1954, where it again proved curiously ahead of its time; a situation not helped by an advertising campaign describing it as the 'X Certificate Musical', which attracted audiences unable in the event to appreciate its qualities and scared off others who could and should.

Pal Joey was Lorenz Hart's own favourite among their shows. He knew rather too well the seamier side of life which it dissected, and the relief he found there from the stresses of a highly complex and troubled personality had by now undermined his physical and mental health to the point where a working partnership was in truth becoming one of 'permanent irritation' and recurrent crisis for a long-suffering but always loyal and devoted Rodgers. Their last show, *By Jupiter*, was written under the strain of these difficulties at their worst, and while it proved as successful as any, there are grounds for the snide comment sometimes made that it is a poor man's *Boys from Syracuse*, despite the presence in the score of 'Careless Rhapsody' and 'Wait Till You See Her'.

And now, seventeen years after *The Garrick Gaieties,* the Theatre Guild again entered the scene; this time with the proposal that Rodgers & Hart make a musical out of Lynn Riggs' bucolic folk-play, *Green Grow the Lilacs.* Hart wearily declined. The West for him ended 'Way out West on West End Avenue'. Rodgers, however, was intrigued, and with Hart's blessing took the idea to Oscar Hammerstein II, with results that opened another era under the title of *Oklahoma!*

One credit more remained to the old alliance; a revival of *A Connecticut Yankee* for which they wrote several new numbers. Even here, at the end of his road, Hart could still work wonders with the most everyday words and sentiments in 'Can't You Do a Friend a Favour', and send everyone home laughing over that lethal lay of Arthurian England, 'To Keep My Love Alive', in which Queen Morgan-Le-Fay mordantly reflects:

> I caught Sir James with his protectoress
> The rector's wife, I mean the rectoress.
> His heart stood still—angina pectoris.

Lorenz Hart died a few days after the revival opened in New York, at the age of forty-eight, on November 22, 1943.

Nearly thirty years after Hart's death Rodgers & Hart not only remain in the public ear; they have acquired an additional cult status among the *aficionados,* who avidly seek out and relish their less familiar facets. Yet they have never taken on the obvious period flavour of so many of their contemporaries in popular music. We go on listening to the tunes because they are good tunes; not because they are quaintly evocative of times past. The words likewise retain their freshness. Hart's jokes are still pungent, his strain of melancholy perhaps touching the emotions of the 'seventies even more closely than those of his own generation. As they once said, most melodically, 'Painters of pictures, writers of books, never could tell the half' in assessing them in mere prose. You have to listen, and you do.

The Barrison Sisters

BY PHILIP KAPLAN

WHEN the Five Barrison Sisters brought their act to Berlin's Wintergarten stage in 1896 they took the sophisticated Berliners by surprise. Here was a new kind of sex show, fresh and provocative, for the five fluffy-headed blondes in rush bonnets and girlish pinafores made it clear from the start that they were not so innocent as they appeared.

The *Meine Kleine Katz* number captivated the audience immediately with its charming blend of innocence and innuendo. As the curtain rose a few feet off the stage floor, five sets of frilly white petticoats appeared from beneath five demurely raised pinafores. From behind the curtain five girlish voices sang invitingly, 'Would you like to see my pussy?' The curtain continued to rise, and now each Barrison Sister raised her petticoats higher and higher, repeating her tantalising invitation. Then, with an impudent grin, she lowered the front edge of frill—and a bewildered *kitten* peered out from her gathered skirts.

The Five Barrison Sisters—Lona, Sophia, Inger, Olga and Gertrude—had brought a refreshing new sex image to Europe. In their schoolgirl costumes, the Barrisons were far removed from the famous Tingle-Tangle Girls of the international variety shows, who wore velour roses in their dyed hair, corsets to accentuate their breasts, and tights that revealed a good deal more than promises. By contrast, the Barrisons' appeal lay in a clever combination of innocence and precocious sexuality. Although their childish songs were quite banal, the girls' impudent smiles teased each lyric into a shining prophecy. What made the Barrison Sisters so unusual was their exuberance, their willingness to be 'shameless', and their apparent delight with themselves and the audience. Their costumes were well chosen for virginal effect: white bib blouses, black pleated skirts, short white socks and buttoned shoes. But underneath that innocent schoolgirl attire—white frilly knickers with naughty black garters. How their audiences loved sharing that secret with them!

Overnight, the Five Barrison Sisters were a sensation. The famous *Art Nouveau* artist, Thomas Th. Heine, was one of the first to catch their spirit, and his delightful drawings in turn inspired the *Jugendstil* period. The writer Anton Lindner analysed the Barrison Sisters' success in his book *Die Barrisons, Ein Kunstraum, Zeitsatire,* published in Berlin in 1897. Although he called their high-pitched voices squeaky and their legs rubbery, Lindner was charmed by the sense of joy the Barrisons communicated to their enthusiastic audiences. By showing the audiences that they were having fun, Lindner declared, the Barrison Sisters exposed the great lie of virtue in the sexual hypocrisy of the times. What matter if they lacked the grace of a Taglioni or a Grisi—there was something fascinating and new in the dancing of the Barrisons.

Drawings of the Barrison Sisters by Thomas Th. Heine

Neither acrobatic nor aesthetic, their dancing was direct and clear—and modern.

Eager to get into the act, newspapers vied for intimate details of the little darlings' rise to fame. They recounted how their Danish father had arrived in New York in 1885 with his wife and six children. Although seeking his fortune in America, Lyceus Kyritz didn't realise he was actually bringing it with him. Even at the Immigration Office, it was reported, the five adorable Kyritz girls had attracted a great deal of attention as they stood in a row beside Papa.

The family soon settled down in a poor quarter of Brooklyn, where Papa Kyritz worked mending umbrellas and carving ivory handles. A strict father, he kept a sharp eye on his bevy— especially Lona, the oldest. She had already had some stage experience in Denmark, and could do a charming little dance and recite engagingly. At sixteen, Lona was an outstanding beauty, well developed and temperamental.

In the autumn of 1889 Mama Kyritz heard that Owen Feree was looking for little girls to feature in his forthcoming production of *The Fairy's Well*. Mama persuaded Papa to take the children for an audition. The five fluffy-headed dolls with their big, blue eyes and saucy grins were hired on the spot. At this early point in their careers the girls changed their name to 'The Barrison Sisters'.

Their next appearance was in *Cinderella*, a typical musical revue of the day. When the Barrisons appeared on stage, holding kittens in their arms, the audience whistled. When they sat astride five broomsticks, playfully exposing their black-stockinged legs, the audience cheered. Lona Barrison added to the excitement with an impudent rendition of 'Daddy Wouldn't Buy Me A Bow-Wow'. Then, called back for encores, the girls delighted everyone by taking their bows with their backsides to the audience and their skirts raised.

Taking advantage of their sensational publicity, William Fleron, Broadway's greatest press agent, hired the Barrison Sisters for his production of *Mr Cupid*. A handsome dandy in yellow kid gloves, silk hat and tails, Fleron proved to be a real Mr Cupid when he married Lona Barrison shortly after the show opened.

The five sisters
Barrison in Paris,
1896, when they
appeared at the
Folies-Bergère.
*Harvard Theatre
Collection.*

THE BEVY
On the right are
the Barrison
Sisters as they
appeared in New
York in 1892.
There were only
four sisters in the
act at the
beginning.
*Harvard Theatre
Collection.*

On the left is reproduced a colour lithograph (in Mr Philip Kaplan's collection) illustrating the Five Barrison Sisters as they appeared in Berlin singing their famous song, *Meine Kleinen Katz*. Above it is a photograph taken in Paris in 1896, when the sisters were appearing at the Folies-Bergère, one of whose posters for the act is reproduced on this page.

Photographs of Sophia (left) and Lona (right) in their 'teens.

Under the guidance of this indefatigable and ingenious manager the Barrison Sisters appeared in many successful New York revues over the next few years. But by 1895 the girls were beset with the problems of adolescence. They were getting tall and skinny, outgrowing their baby fat and sassy charm. Only Lona's beauty and cleverness saved the act. Besides their other worries, the younger Barrison girls were plagued by the Society for the Prevention of Cruelty to Children, which had caught up with the troupe and was now making bookings hard to find.

At this point Fleron decided it was time to seek fresh pastures for his lambs. Under his protective wing the Barrison Sisters left for Europe, stopping first in London. There they were wildly applauded for their song-and-dance act in English schoolgirl uniforms. From London, on to Berlin and the Wintergarten stage. Well publicised by Fleron, with provocative posters and suggestive photographs plastered everywhere, the Sisters played the Wintergarten for eight full months.

Fresh from their Berlin triumph the Barrisons headed for Paris, where in a short time they monopolised the stage of the Folies-Bergère. The sophisticated French audiences, who had seen countless dressing and undressing scenes, were enthralled. Parisians were tired of getting-up scenes, going-to-bed scenes, bathroom adventures, honeymoon intimacies, flea-hunting expeditions and sleep-walking surprises. They were ready for something new—and roly-poly, pretty-faced Lona Barrison gave it to them!

Lona, the cleverest of the sisters, also had the best theatrical imagination. In one of the acts that made her famous Lona came on stage in a man's dress suit. Discarding the outfit piece by piece, she sang a mocking ditty about the discomforts of men's clothing. When she had finally removed the starched linen dress shirt, last of the costume to go, she stood in a gaily-striped silk chemise that reached from her throat to the middle of each pink-stockinged thigh. And now, she announced to the delighted audience, she was suitably attired for riding! A horse was brought out on stage, Lona mounted him in grand style, and around the stage she went, singing a song of the delights of riding astride (rather than the uncomfortable side-saddle position favoured by the women of the time). Although one critic later remarked that the horse looked ashamed of himself, the audience went wild with admiration. *'Vive les américaines!'* they shouted, in an astonishing outburst of non-nationalistic enthusiasm.

Cresting the wave of popularity, Fleron and the girls decided to return to America, confident of continued success. Although the Sisters had many imitators by that time—Les Sisters Machinson, Les Cinq Demie-Vierges and others—none ever equalled the Barrisons' skilful mixture of *naïveté* and sly vulgarity.

In 1898 the troupe returned to New York, where they were immediately booked at the famous Koster & Bials. But New York was not Paris or Berlin. Although they were billed as 'the wickedest girls in the world', the subtleties of the Barrisons' act escaped the New York critics, who complained that the girls sang French songs with an English accent and English songs with a French accent. A popular burlesque act of the time even called itself 'The Embarrassing Sisters in Their Nasty Performance'.

Despite what the critics thought, however, New Yorkers were curious. Night after night they flocked to Koster & Bials, which was reported to be 'crammed, jammed, packed and crowded, with standing room at a premium'. On stage, the girls took encores gleefully, blowing coy kisses to the crowd and hugging each other in a great show of pleasure.

When attendance began to drop at the theatre, William Fleron once again showed his genius for publicity: he announced to the Press that Lona Barrison planned to ride her horse, Maestoso, in the Society Horse Show, the social event of the year. New York's high society buzzed with curiosity. Would Lona ride astride? Would she dare to appear at the event in one of her famous scanty costumes—or in pink tights?! Pleased by the free publicity, the Horse Show Committee declared at first that it had no objection to whatever way Lona chose to ride. But rumours about Lona and her horseback stunt grew wilder and wilder. Was it true she planned to ride *bareback*, wearing silver spurs, her horse naked except for jewelled surcingle? Some feared that Lona would try to outstrip Lady Godiva. When Lona announced she would wear pantalettes for the occasion, the nervous Horse

The Shocking
Performance
of Miss Lona
Barrison at
a New York
Theatre.

'Has Public Taste Sunk to this Degrading Level?' Under this heading the
New York Journal of Sunday, October 11, 1896, printed the drawings above, with
the sub-title: 'If the New York Theatre-goers Unblushingly Flock to See a
Vulgar Young Woman Undress Herself on the Stage, What May We Expect
Next?' Mrs Charlotte Smith is quoted as saying: 'I never saw an exhibition
in any theatre more suggestive, lewd and indecent . . . The elder Barrison
undressed on the stage and gave an exhibition on horseback that was even
more disgraceful than that of her sisters. A law ought to be passed putting a
stop to such exhibitions.'

Show Committee suddenly backed down, declaring that no *outré* costume would be allowed.

From that point on, the Barrison Sisters' decline was surprisingly and sadly swift. New bookings never materialised. Hoping to recapture former triumphs, the troupe returned to Paris with Fleron. But times had changed, and the fickle public had found new loves. Bad luck also contributed to the Barrisons' loss of popularity. A nobleman committed suicide over one of the girls. The troupe was banished from Germany by royal edict after it was revealed that a scandalously large sum of money had been spent on the Barrisons by a member of the royal family. Lona and her faithful Fleron were still to be seen riding around Paris in their rented Victoria, but Lona had grown fat and dowdyish, and her once-beautiful face was now puffy and expressionless.

Papa Kyritz' death in 1907 brought to a climax the bad publicity the Barrisons had been receiving. Newspaper gossip columns disclosed that not a single Barrison sister had come forward to pay the funeral expenses of poor Lyceus Kyritz, father of the five little darlings whose tantalising innocence had so beguiled the world.

Music Hall Memories

BY FRED BASON

N OW THAT the old-fashioned Music Hall has ceased to exist you find intellectual people taking far more interest in it than they ever did in the days when there were twenty or thirty Music Halls putting on twice-nightly shows in London alone—to say nothing of the Grands and Empires and Palaces and Alhambras in the provinces.

I became a Music Hall fan in 1921. Before then I hadn't even the price of a seat in the gallery, which cost fourpence or sixpence. The very first variety star I met in person was Marie Lloyd, who was indeed a great star, though much of her act was above me (or rather *below* me, for I'd been brought up very strictly). I met her at the Camberwell Palace. I was very shy; I held out my autograph book and stuttered, 'Please . . . will you?'

'Come along of me,' she says. 'I'll do it in the dressing room.' She laughed—a fruity laugh, flashing her teeth. In we goes to her little, rather bare dressing room. She puts down a big handbag and takes my little autograph book and pen. 'You've no ink in it!' she says. 'What's the use of a pen with no ink in it?' and she laughs again. However, she runs downstairs, gets a bottle of ink from the stage doorkeeper, fills my cheap fountain pen, and starts writing her name. The ink won't flow and she gives the pen a shake, throwing blots on the page. 'It's shot out too soon,' she says. 'Never mind, I'll sign my name with the blots.' Which she does, writing it bold and clear, and adding *September 26th, 1921*. 'Now hop off,' she says, with another laugh, 'before I get undressed.' Her dresser comes in. 'Hey,' says Marie Lloyd, 'give me one of those pictures of myself.' And she picks one out of a box writes on it *To a little Gent—Marie Lloyd*.

I never saw her again, but I went to her funeral, with several thousand other people, and I wore a black tie for a week. I was fourteen years old.

I saw most of the big Music Hall stars between 1921 and 1931. I was specially fond of Ella Shields, the original singer of 'Burlington Bertie'—so smart and dapper; and Harry Weldon and his wife Hylda Glyder—a very funny man and a sweet singer, wonderful troupers both; and Little Tich. I remember Little Tich with a special affection, though he was always reluctant to sign autographs because he was sensitive about having six fingers on each hand. Still, he gave me a photograph, signed 'Harry Tich'. His real name was Harry Relph, and he was a most intelligent man, who could talk fluently in five languages. Another very intelligent person, though you'd never guess it to see her on stage, was Nellie Wallace.

George Robey was another of my favourite comics, and he was the autograph hunter's delight, because he always carried about with him some pen and ink sketches of himself—drawn by himself—and he'd sign them *Good Luck, Geo Robey*. I asked him once whether he was wishing luck to himself or me. 'We both need it, my boy,' he said. 'It's as draughty at the top of the bill as it is at the back of the gallery. Either of us could come tumbling down —fast!'

I collected hundreds of autographs of Music Hall stars, and I'll show some of them gladly to anyone who calls to see me at 4 Broadmayne, in Portland Street, S.E.17. I remember asking Will Fyffe for his—he was the great Scottish comedian who sang 'I Belong to Glasgow'. He asked me how much his autograph was worth. I said, cheeky-like, 'Well, ten of yours is worth one of Noël Coward's.' 'And who the hell is Noël Coward?' he asked, I was amazed: he really didn't seem to know. This was just before the last war, when Noël Coward was the idol of the West End. 'You might as well ask,' I said, 'who is Ethel M. Dell?' 'And who *is* Ethel M. Dell?' said Will Fyffe. He really didn't know. When I told him she wrote love stories he said, 'Do I look the sort 'o chap to read love stories?' I had to admit he didn't.

I asked Will Fyffe if he really belonged to Glasgow, as the words of the song went. He laughed. 'Na, laddie!' he said. 'The world's my oyster. The only thing Scottish about me is the whisky inside me.' Whether this was true or just a gag I don't know, but he was a great star and a great performer.

But of all my Music Hall stars the one I loved best was Aileen Stanley, the singer of 'Over on the Sunny Side' and 'Souvenirs'— a great gramophone star of the 'twenties. I met her first in

1922 when I was an unkempt urchin shivering on a cold winter's night at the stage door of the Alhambra in Leicester Square. When I asked her for her autograph she carted me off to the Kit Kat Club, a ritzy night-club in the Haymarket, made me eat a hearty supper, and asked me all about myself. She then made me promise to meet her outside Swan & Edgar's in Piccadilly Circus the next morning at ten, when she bought me an entire rig-out of suit, vest, shirt, tie, sock, overcoat and shoes.

'Now you look a perfect English gentleman,' she said. 'You can come and work for me.' There followed two of the happiest years of my life. My chief job was to buy bottles of the very finest port, and stand in the wings with about two fingers of port in a clean glass. She'd drink this just before she went on to sing three or four songs in her very individual American voice—a voice with a cherry in it. Then she'd come off stage and drink another finger of port before singing her encore. This drink was entirely medicinal, as a protection against the smoke in the theatre and the fog outside. Somehow it lubricated her vocal cords.

She was a very beautiful woman, and is still a very good friend. I heard from her in America in December 1969, when she ordered a copy of THE SATURDAY BOOK and sent me some dollars to buy myself a Christmas cake. When I wrote and thanked her I said she ought to come to London and let me look after her as I'd done when I was fifteen. She sent me her love, but said she couldn't come because she couldn't leave her dog. Lucky dog!

But it wasn't only the stars that attracted me to the Music Hall. Some of my favourite acts must be totally forgotten nowadays. There was Khartoum, the Persian Pianist, with a very dark complexion, and a turban. He entered a darkened stage, made a profound bow, and played divinely, with lots of flourishes and trills and runs up and down the keys. I thought him the height of romance until one night I asked him for his autograph at the stage door and he spat out in cockney: 'Get aht of the bleedin' way.' I'm afraid the only Persian he'd ever seen was a carpet.

Then there was Tucker, the Singing Violinist, who both played and sang, and wore a flowing tie. He accepted applause by ducking his head and opening both ends of his tie—a most singular trick. I have an idea that he is now Charles Tucker, an agent.

And I liked too the Luminous Latins, who painted their clothes and guitars with luminous paint, and when the lights from the 'gods' were switched on to them they looked like coloured ghosts.

And here's another memory, which I've recalled before, but I'll let you have it again as it rounds off my Music Hall memories and concerns a 'turn' which used to be a great favourite of the Editor's. I was waiting at the stage door of the Holborn Empire for Max Miller, the wonderful, irrepressible, and shockingly Cheeky Chappie, when out of the door came a sad-looking, elderly man, whom I didn't recognise. Assuming he was an artiste, I held out my autograph book. 'Do you really want my autograph?' he asked. 'Yes, sir,' I said. So he signed and said, 'Would you like a signed photograph too?' 'I'd be delighted,' I replied.

Out of a shabby wallet he drew a dog-eared photograph, already signed and dated. 'Thank you very much,' I said. 'Thank *you*,' he said. 'Thank you for asking me. I've been carrying that photo round for quite a while, hoping someone would ask me for my autograph. I thought I was a back-number.' Then he put his hand in his pocket and gave me seven shillings. I said I really didn't want it. But he said: 'I promised myself some time ago that when next someone asked me for my autograph I'd give him or her all the money I had in my right-hand trousers pocket. Actually you're not lucky, you know. You're rather unlucky, because a few hours ago I had over ten pounds in that pocket, but I've lost nearly all of it this evening, playing poker. Take advice from an old man: never play cards for money.'

That advice came from Sam Mayo, one of the vintage stars of the British Music Hall, who wore a red wig and a shabby old dressing gown, and sat at a piano with a lugubrious expression singing sardonic songs in a curious whining voice. He had been at the top of the bill when I was a child in arms.

Astaire

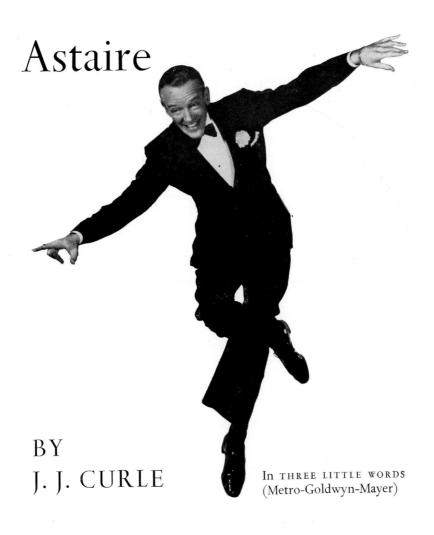

BY
J. J. CURLE

In THREE LITTLE WORDS
(Metro-Goldwyn-Mayer)

EXACT upon the beat,
machine-gun-fire staccato
tapping feet
exteriorise,
then STOP!—Slow smile
extending Laurel's mouth,
the gesture's style
dissolves from face to arm,
from arm to wrist:
the ordinary can again exist.

In BLUE SKIES
with Bing Crosby
(Paramount)

Wɪᴛʜ light, flat voice,
cracked-edged,
with down-thrust hands
and slightly simian stoop
(the 'parachutist lands'
posture of set-to-go),

In LET'S DANCE
with Betty Hutton
(Paramount)

the turning head
moved square to camera,
its features dead-
pan, save the twisted-up
self-mocking lips
(a cartoon-scribbled face),

In DADDY LONG LEGS
with Leslie Caron
(Twentieth-Century Fox)

frame without hips,
(the waiter humbly glad
of coming tips)
he plugs half-bitter quips.

In YOU'LL NEVER GET RICH
with Rita Hayworth
(Columbia)

AND then—
the music takes him,
shakes him,
wakes him,
with its stark electric shock.
A force that drives
arrives ecstatic,
acrobatic,
breaks time's clock;

In TOP HAT
with Ginger Rogers (R.K.O.)

thrills to find,
to touch and grace
upon all nature's
tender face
the convolutions
lovers trace
in learning features
loving-long
(like hands
that mould them into song).

In THE BAND WAGGON
With Cyd Charisse
(Metro-Goldwyn-Mayer)

Exact,
    percussive,
balanced,
swung,
his body is
the censer slung
upon a chain
that brings it back
(all movement reined
within its slack),
inevitable and precise,
a gyroscopic, centred force
that can be hurtled through two planes

In BROADWAY MELODY
OF 1940
with Eleanor Powell
(Metro-Goldwyn-Mayer)

but on a third holds changeless course.
About some point that flows in space
he moves, contained,
in whiplash grace,
an easy panther, pattering claws
through multiples
of motion's laws;
a man unfettered,
born to thrive
on simple zest
of being alive;

In EASTER PARADE
with Judy Garland
(Metro-Goldwyn-Mayer)

a force of nature
with a grin,
immune to death
and time and sin,
because where it
contrives to be
verges upon
eternity.

In EASTER PARADE
with Ann Miller
(Metro-Goldwyn-Mayer)

AND THEN—
from thrust
and power
and beat,
from pistol shots
of triggered feet,
the music opens,
slows and sings;
legs shadow out
to skaters' rings

In THE SKY'S THE LIMIT
with Joan Leslie (R.K.O.)

as arms encircle,
bodies glide,
sails ghosting
one unrippled tide.

In SECOND CHORUS
with Paulette Goddard
(Paramount)

PRECISION still,
but flexed and smoothed,
a theorem set out
not proved,
inevitably bound
to flow,

—exact, unwearied,
even, slow,
from premise
to fulfilment. He
moves with an adept's
ecstasy,

In HOLIDAY INN
with Marjorie Reynolds
(Paramount)

withdrawn, remote;
the face
at last

In ROBERTA
with Ginger Rogers
(R.K.O.)

more sadly,
almost nobly
cast.

In THREE LITTLE
WORDS
with Vera Ellen
(Metro-Goldwyn-
Mayer)

AND WE who watch
observe a rite
in which we cannot
ever quite
explain to others
what we see.

THIS IS ART's central mystery;
    to be at once
the means and end;
what facts achieve,
what they portend.
Here is an artist:
—if you care
that such exist,
hail Fred Astaire!

In YOLANDA ANI
THE THIEF
with Lucille Brem
(Metro-Goldwyn-
Mayer)

LADIES' COTTON SHIRTS.

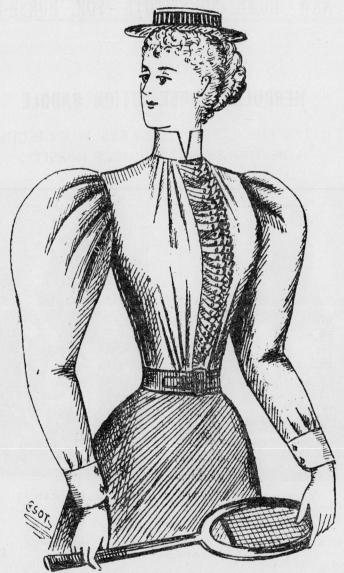

Zephyr Shirt, in Pink, Blue, or Heliotrope, with Double Hemstitched Frill, Stiff Collar and Cuffs, 3/11.

Special Illustrated Sheet of all the Newest Shapes in Shirts and Blouses sent on application.

Orders by Post carefully executed. Patterns of all goods Post Free,

Harrods, 1895

THE NEW HOME SUBSTITUTE FOR HORSE-RIDING.

THE
HERCULES HORSE-ACTION SADDLE

STIMULATES THE LIVER, QUICKENS THE CIRCULATION AIDS DIGESTION, REDUCES OBESITY.

APPROVED AND ADOPTED BY THE ROYAL FAMILY.

PRICE LIST.

QUALITY **A.**— Extra mounted and fitted; internal arrangements guaranteed to last 10 years **£19 17 6**

QUALITY **B.**—Pigskin or Morocco Saddles, with Leather sides and best Nickel-plated fittings; internal arrangements guaranteed to last 8 years **17 0 0**

QUALITY **C.**—Morocco Saddles, with American Cloth sides; internal arrangements guaranteed to last 6 years **14 5 0**

OTHER QUALITIES.—Full sized, **£11 7/0**; medium size, **£9 9/0**; small size, **£6 10/0.**

(1895)

PEAKE'S PORTABLE SLEEPING REST

FOR

RAILWAY TRAVELLERS.

Sleeping Rest, as Illustration.

Length when folded, 36 inches. Breadth, 3½ inches.

Price, 4/9 each.

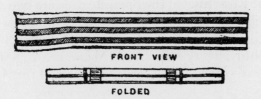

FRONT VIEW

FOLDED

All the above are delivered Carriage free, subject to the Conditions set forth on page 4.

(1895)

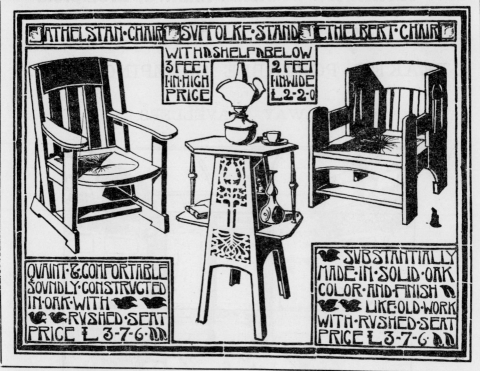

T HE GREATEST INNOVATOR in London's shopping of the nineteenth century was probably Arthur Liberty, who was so impressed by the oriental importations displayed at the great International Exhibition in London in 1862 that he was put in charge of an 'Oriental Warehouse' by his employers, Messrs Farmer & Rogers, of Regent Street. He subsequently launched out on his own in 1875.

Liberty's played an immensely important part in the development of taste and the Aesthetic Movement. William Morris was a patron of the shop, as were Carlyle, Ruskin, Whistler, Watts, Millais and the Rossettis. On the opposite page are two advertisements from Liberty's catalogue of 1883—the earliest that has been preserved—which indicate the Grecian and Indian influences to which Arthur Liberty responded. Above is a page from the catalogue of 1898, when Liberty's were pioneers of the *Art Nouveau* movement.

quarters; a slight variation being sometimes required in the position of the latter loops, as the figure to be fitted is longer or shorter in the waist than the standard.

In arranging the drapery upon the person, the two inner loops—those at the quarters—are to be passed over buttons affixed to the underdress, the place of which must be well on the shoulder, a little to the front. It is to be understood that the centre of the shawl forms the back of the garment. When these two loops have been fastened to the buttons, that half of the width of the shawl which will be hanging between the shoulders must be drawn together, and may be permanently tacked at the waist, below which a portion of it will then fall, in the manner of the hood of a burnous. This gives those graceful folds and the additional length at the back of the skirt, to be seen in our woodcut. The folds which form the skirt behind must now be drawn well back from the hips, and to facilitate this a pin may be inserted to bring them together beneath that portion of the edge of the shawl which has been tacked at the waist. The corner hanging from the left shoulder has now to be passed beneath the left arm, and, crossing the chest, to be fastened by its loop to the right-hand button; the same action reversed being afterwards employed for the corresponding side. The two ends of the long shawl will now be crossing the chest, and it needs only the zone

to secure the drapery in its place, that on the left being gathered into the hand as the zone is put on, and allowed to hang over it. Some measure of taste and a knowledge of the hang of classical draperies are necessary to the due arrangement of this sort of pocket, which, though not essential, is still desirable, as giving to the skirt in front the beautiful oblique folds which will be seen in the engravings.

This arrangement, which takes so long to describe, can be acccomplished on the person in two minutes with moderate skill and practice; but where the skill is consciously deficient, a few stitches judiciously placed would suffice to attach the drapery to the underdress as a permanent tunic or polonaise, the passing of the loops over the buttons being all that would be left to do if the pocket was also dispensed with. Although the drapery would then forego one of its distinctive merits, of being capable of being folded into a small compas, without fear of crushing, it would still form a graceful garment of incomparably easy production, hanging in natural folds, the weight of which would, according to another principle of all good dress, be borne from the shoulder. That the dress here treated of could be richly adorned with embroidery, or even lace, is evident, while it is equally apparent that the essential beauty of all clothing resides in it, irrespective of such addition. It is thus suited to a wide range of needs and means.—*Queen, 10th Jan.,* 1880.

Pattern of Dress 2/7; of Under Dress 2/1.

WATERPROOF COATS and INVERNESS CAPES.

COATS.

WOOL CAPE.
50, 52, 54, 56
inches long.

CARNARVON.
27 in. Cape all Round, or
Regulation, see Inverness
Capes.

4/- Extra.

With 17 in. Detached
Capes.

4/6 Extra.

8/6 ,,

INVERNESS CAPES.
48, 50, 52, 54, 56
inches long.

COATS	50	52	54	56
Strong Twill Black Proof	11/6	11/9	12/3	13/9
Black Cashmere ..	22/6	23/6	24/6	25/6
Fancy Tweeds and Checks	18/6	19/6	20/6	21/6
Extra Fine, all Wool ..	23/6	25/-	26/6	28/-
Superior, all Wool, Scotch Mixtures ..	30/-	31/6	33/-	34/6
Superior Box Cloths ..	38/6	42/-	44/6	47/-

INVERNESS CAPES	48	50	52	54	56
Black Cashmere Velvet Collar	16/9	16/9	16/9	16/9	16/
Superior Quality, lined Red, Black, or Check ..	21/-	21/-	21/-	21/-	21
Black Cashmere Extra Fine	30/6	31/6	32/6	33/6	34/
„ „ Extra Superfine	37/6	37/6	37/6	37/6	37/
Woollen Check..	27/-	28/6	30/-	32/-	33,
All Wool Scotch Tweeds ..	33/	35/6	37/-	38/6	40/

B Y WAY OF CONTRAST to the aestheticism of Liberty's and the luxury of Victoria and Knightsbridge the store of A. W Gamage was established in High Holborn to provide for the more mundane needs of the City clerk and business man. The appeal was essentially masculine. 'The Athlete's Provider' specialised in sports goods, cycling kit, men's wear, and mechanical contrivances.

The illustrations above and opposite are from the earliest of Gamage's catalogues we have been able to find, published in 1893. Thereafter the catalogue was expanded every year, until it contained a prodigious variety not only of sporting requisites but also household goods, machinery, conjuring tricks and toys. Indeed, during the second decade of the twentieth century the arrival of Gamage's Catalogue, early in October, was the joyful harbinger of Christmas for many thousands of children throughout Great Britain.

BOOT & SHOE DEPARTMENT.

HE DERBY WATERPROOF ALL HORSE-SKIN BOOT.

Hand-sewn—

16/6   18/6   21/-   25/-

KID LEG-BUTTON BOOT,

Patent Leather, Horse-skin, or French Calf, Kid Top,

10/6   12/6   14/6

Warranted.

STOUT WALKING BOOT,

For Town or Country wear—

All Horse-skin or French Calf,

10/6 12/6 16/6 18/6.

Waterproof.

HE M.C. LACE SIDE-SPRING,

In Horse Skin or Calf, Kid Top.

Sewn,   12/6   14/6   16/6

and-Sewn,   16/6   18/6   21/-

THE BROQUE LACE BOOT.

Best Hand-Sewn, Patent Leather,

Horse Skin or Calf, 18/6 21/- 25/-

Russia Leather, 21/-, 25/- Hand-Sewn.

THE PARK BOOT.

Cloth Legs, in Patent or Horse Skin,

Sewn,   18/6   21/-   22/6

Best Hand-Sewn,   25/-

ATENT LEATHER GOLOSH BUTTON BOOT, Kid Top.

ith Seams at Sides, 10/6, 12/6, 14/6—Sewn.

itto, without Seams at Sides, 16/6, 18/6, 21/-
Hand-Sewn.

SIDE-SPRING BOOT,

In Patent Leather, Horse Skin or French Calf,
Kid Top,

10/6   12/6   14/6.

Hand-sewn, Plain or Toecaps, 16/9, 18/6, 21/-.

THE MOCK BUTTON SIDE-SPRING,

In Patent Leather, Horse Skin or Calf,

10/6   12/6   14/6.

Hand-Sewn,   16/6   18/6   21/-

THE PARK LACE BOOT,

Brown Ooze Calf or Russia Leather.

Russia Leather, 10/6, 12/6, 14/6.

Ooze Calf, 12/6, 14/6, 16/6, 18/6.

WARRANTED

GENTS' LINEN GAITERS,

For Summer Wear.

In White Drill, Straw or Grey Colors—

From 2/6. Cloth 2/11.

THE STOUT TOWN BOOT.

Real Hand-Sewn, in Horse Skin, Kid Top,

12/6   14/6   16/6   18/6   20/9

No Combination.

Gamage's, 1893

Edison Bell Phonographs.

The New Gem Phonograph.

This New Machine is fitted with a Recorder, as well as a Reproducer, Chip Brush, Trumpet and Handsome Bent Wood Cabinet, which completely encloses the Instrument, and forms a convenient carrying case as well as protecting the Machine, when not in use. The Machine is improved in several points of detail and is really a first-class all-round Phonograph—with it you can make your own Records.

Gamage's Price .. 49 6

List Price, £3

Edison Home Phonograph.

Enclosed in Handsome Oak Case with accessories as above and equipped with a Spring Motor, that runs six records with a single winding.

Gamage's Price .. £7 5 0

List Price £7 10 0

The New Standard Phonograph.

EDISON-BELL "Standard" Phonograph, with Clockwork Spring Motor, inclosed in Handsome Oak Carrying Case, with Automatic Reproducer and Recorder, Shaver for surfacing cylinders, Nickel Horn, Camel-Hair Chip Brush, Winding Key, Book of Instructions and list of records.

Runs six records with single winding.

Gamage's Price, £4 19s. 6d.

List Price, £5 5s.

Price 2/6 Each

A RECORD CANNOT BE BROKEN

Pric 25 D

Post

PHONOGRAPH ACCESSORIES.

Edison-Bell Wax Records, 1/- each, 12/- doz. Post Free.   Blank Cylinders, 7½d. each, 7/- doz.
Concert Records, 4/6 each.   Pathe Records, 1/- each, 12/- doz. Post Free.
Clifford Records, 10½d. each, 9/- doz.   Postage, &c., 6d.

	Gamage's Price.	List Price.
Micro Attachment for Standard Phonograph	£2 2 0	£2 5 0
Bettini Attachment for Home Phonograph ..	4 4 0	4 10 0
Blank Cylinders, for Edison Concert Phonograph	0 3 0	0 3 6
Cylinder Tray	0 1 10	0 2 0
Hearing Tubes, per Way	0 1 10	0 2 0
Diaphragm Glasses	0 0 2	0 0 6
Cloth Covered Case, to hold 12 Cylinders	0 9 11	0 10 6
Do. do. 24 Cylinders	0 16 6	0 17 6
Do. do. 36 Cylinders ..	1 2 6	1 5 0
Do. do. 12 Cylinders with space for accessories ..	1 0 0	1 1 0
Cardboard Boxes, to hold 6 Cylinders	0 0 11	0 1 0
Do. Do. 12 Cylinders ..	0 1 4½	0 1 6
Diaphragm for Graphophone	0 6 6	
The "Rex"	0 10 0	
Extra Loud Speaking Automatic Diaphragm for Standard and Home Phonographs ..	0 15 6	1 2 6

	Gamage's Price.	List P
Gallery and Tubes complete for 15 persons, with flexible connection for Type No. 4 Machine	£2 5 0	2 1
Gallery and Tubes complete for 12 persons, with flexible connection for Type No. 2 Machine	1 17 6	2
Celluloid Nickel Ear Cups, per pair ..	0 3 3	0
"Y" Pieces and Ear Pieces	0 0 2½	0
Oil, per bottle	0 0 5	

The Cheapest House in the Trade for—

Seamless Brass Horns.

14-in.	18-in.	24-in. by 11½-in.	31-in. by 13½	42-in. by 16½-in.	56.
3/9	7/6	10/6	13/9	30/-	6

Aluminium Trumpet 8-in Bell, 3 6   10-in. 5 6
Folding Bronze Stands with Carrying Arm 4

A. W. GAMAGE, Ltd, will not be responsible for damage to Records in transit (Post or otherwise) but take every precaution to have them securely packed. Carriage extra on all Goods on this page outside London Carrier Radius.

Cinematographs.

Directions for Working Cinematographs.

Having adjusted the lamp and placed the lantern in position, the film to be exhibited is placed on the reel over the front of the lantern, which is then swung open on its hinge to admit the film. This is placed in position, the little teeth in the sprocket wheel engaging with the holes in the sides of the film. The front is then closed again, and held tight by the spring catch

The film is supplied in a continuous band, and will now be shown on the screen, immediately the handle on the side of the lantern body is turned the pictures will rapidly replace each other, producing the animated effect. The height of the top reel can be adjusted as required, and should hold the band of the film comfortably in position.

No. 790 Cinematograph.
SPECIFICATION.

New pattern cinematograph, with japanned tin body, powerful oil lamp, Russian iron chimney, all thoroughly well made, and guaranteed to give good results; will exhibit either cinematograph pictures or ordinary lantern slides, with slight adjustment of the front. The case is divided up, as illustrated, with space for films, and rack for the slides.

Price 18/6 complete in fine wood box with 3 films and 12 glass lantern slides.

No. 791 Cinematograph.

Thoroughly serviceable table cinematograph, being well made throughout in enamelled iron and brass, the films are standard Edison Gauge. Fittings are also supplied for using ordinary lantern slides, which must be two inches wide.

Price 25/- complete, with 6 films and 12 two inch slides, packed in strong wood case

Improved Black Japanned Body.

The Body is made of tin, japanned black, with Russian iron chimney, all brass fittings, powerful oil lamp, mounted on wood base, and fitted with extra front for use with ordinary slides.

MECHANISM. - Is in brass, and is actuated by a large fly wheel and spring-wire band; it is made to take the Standard Edison gauge films, and full length films can be exhibited if required. This Lantern can be used as a magic lantern.

FILMS.—Three are supplied with each instrument, highly coloured, and of very superior quality, also 12 glass slides.

Price 12 6 complete with 3 Films.

Extra Films, Price 1/- er or 5 6

SERIES I.	SERIES II.	SERIES III.
...ker.	Fencing School.	A Good Little Dog.
...sherwoman.	Serpentine Dance.	Gymnastic Exercises.
...sure Drive.	Minuet.	Two Clowns.
...ampions.	Juggler.	An Exercise.
...ors.	A Smoker.	A Conjurer.
...s in the Streets.	A Horse Race.	The Interrupted Dinner.

No. 792 Up-to-date Cinematographs.

Well Finished Frame, is made of Oxydised Russian Iron mounted on strong Wooden ..e, will take Edison Gauge Films, and is also fitted with extra front for use as magic ...tern. Specially selected Lense, powerful Duplex Oil Lamp and Reflector.

Complete with 1 Photographic Film and 12 Glass Lantern Slides. Price, C3

For extra Films see page 181.

Combination Cinematograph and Lecture Lantern.

For use with Incandescent Gas, Acetylene, Limelight or Oil Lamp.
Will take Regular Edison Gauge Films.

SPECIFICATION.

MECHANISM.—Standard Edison Gauge sprocket, improved Geneva escapement with shutter and spring film stage.

OPTICS.—A specially made double achromatic Petzval Combination, 2 in. focus, in brass rack and pinion jacket fitted to the cinematograph, and an 8-in. Double Achromatic Lens in rack and pinion mount with flashing shutter fitted for the lecture lantern, and 4-diam. plano-convex condenser.

BODY.—Russian iron, with door and brass sight-hole, cowl and tray, on well-finished walnut base-board with sliding adjustment for the lantern body to be centred, alternately with the cinematograph and with the lecture lantern.

Strong cabinet with strap handle. Price complete (lamp or jet extra) £4 19s. 6d.

Suitable for small Entertainments; will Exhibit Films and Title Slides, or suit a Lantern Lecture.

Best Quality Lamp or Set 7/6 extra.

Gamage's, 1902

GAMAGE'S MODELS OF ENGLIS LOCOMOTIVES (Steam).

Great Central Locomotive with Tender.

No. 7090. Gauge 2.

Beautifully japanned, with oxydized br boiler, 2 oscillating brass cylinders ins frame, brass flanged wheels, brass dome w starting cock, safety valve, bell whistle, br outlet tap, with practical frame guard a brass hand rails, exhaust steam passing throu funnel, japanned tender.

21 ins. long including tender; 6 ins. hig

Price **42/-**

Great Northern Railway Locomotive with Tender.

With Fixed Cylinders and Reversing Gear.

No. 7094. Gauge 2.

Finely japanned, with strong oxydized brass boiler, double action slide valve cylinders, with reversing gear, smoke box, brass steam dome with starting cock, bell whistle, safety valve, and outlet tap, exhaust steam passing through the funnel, Tender mounted on 2 four-wheeled bogie carriages, finely finished.

22 ins. long including Tender.

Price **63/-**

London & South Western Railw Locomotive with Tender.
No. 7098. Gauge 3.
With Fixed Cylinders and Reversing Ge

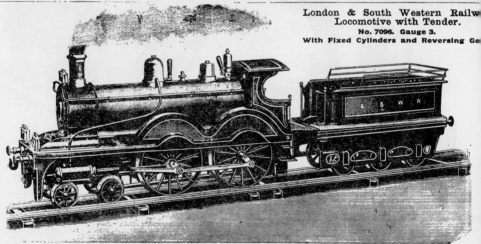

Finely finished, with oxydized brass boiler, double action slide valve cylinders, reversing gear, flame guard, nickelled flanged wheels and connecting ro smoke box, brass domes, safety valve, bell whistle, water gauge, brass starting cock, outlet tap, hand rails and brass spring buffers, exhaust steam passing throu funnel. Tender, finely japanned and elegantly finished, with spring buffers. 28 ins. long including Tender. 8 ins. high. Price **£4 17. 6.**

Gamage's, 1902

WAR! WAR! WAR!

BUY YOUR SONS

SOLDIERS of the KING and BOER SOLDIERS,

Which will enable them to learn THE ART OF MODERN WARFARE.

A. W. GAMAGE Ltd. have the LARGEST COLLECTION of TOY SOLDIERS (English and Foreign) in Great Britain, and an IMMENSE STOCK of **Guns, Cannon, Forts, Swords, Tents, Ambulances, Armour Sets, Armoured Trains, &c., &c., &c., at**

PRICES that will DEFY COMPETITION.

SOLDIERS OF THE KING.—*MADE IN LONDON. Designed and Modelled by First-class English Artists, and produced entirely by British Labour.* **6d. Boxes, 4½d.,** postage 2d. **1/- Boxes, 10½d.,** postage 2d.

THEY are made exact to scale, that is, a foot soldier is the same size as a horse soldier, and the Horses are in proportion to the men, whilst the uniforms and colorings have been most carefully considerea so as to give a correct representa tion of the various regiments.

No. 1B 1st Life Guards ... 4½d.
,, 6B 2nd Dragoon (Scots Greys)... 4½d.
,, 10B 11th Hussars ... 4½d.
,, 12B 16th Lancers (Active Service)... 4½d.
,, 20B Manchester Regt.... 4½d.
,, 21B Northumberland Fusiliers (Active Service Order) ... 4½d.

No. 13B 17th Lancers ... 4½d.
,, 15B Mounted Infantry .. 4½d.
All these have Movable Arms.
No. 16B Coldstream Guards 4½d.
,, 22B Blue Jackets (H.M.'s Navy) ... 4½d.
,, 17B Lancashire Fusiliers 4½d.
,, 23B Cameron Highlandrs 4½d.
Postage 2d.

OUR INDIAN ARMY.

No. 67 Madras Native Infantry 10½d.
,, 66 Bombay Lancers ... 10½d.
,, 46 10th Bengal Lancers... 10½d.
,, 68 2nd Bombay Native Infy. 10½d.
,, 19 West India Regiment 10½d.
,, 45 3rd. Madras Light Cavly. 10½d.

No. 47 1st Bengal Cavalry ... 10½d.
,, 62 1st Bengal Cavalry (10 large mounted soldiers) 1/9
,, 63 10th Bengal Lancers (10 large mounted soldiers) 1/9
Postage 3d.

No. 43 2nd Life Guards ... 10½d.
,, 1 1st Life Guards ... 10½d.
,, 31 1st Dragoon Guards 10½d.
,, 2 Royal Horse Guards 10½d.
,, 32 2nd Dragoon Guards (R. Scots Greys) ... 10½d.
,, 77 Gordon Highlanders and Pipers ... 10½d.
,, 34 Grenadier Guards 10½d.
,, 7 7th Royal Fusiliers 10½d.
,, 99 The 13th Hussars 10½d.
,, 13 3rd Hussars (King's Own) ... 10½d.
,, 12 11th Hussars (Prince Albert's Own) ... 10½d.
,, 23 5th Lancers (R. Irish) 10½d.
,, 24 9th ,, (Queen's R.) 10½d.
,, 18 Worcesters're Reg. 10½d.
,, 16 The Buffs (East Kent Regiment) ... 10½d.

No. 15. **Argyle and Sutherland Highlanders** (Princess Louise's 91st) 10½d.

No. 11 The Black Watch (Royal Highlanders) ... ... 10½d.
,, 91 United States Infantry ... ... 10½d.
,, 92 Spanish Infantry ... ... 10½d.
,, 84 Types of British Army, containing 2nd Life Guards and 7th Royal Fusiliers ... ... 10½d.
,, 81 17th Lancers (Active Service Order) ... ... 10½d.
,, 82 Colors and Pioneers of the Scots Guards ... ... 10½d.
,, 77 Gordon Highlanders and Pipers ... ... 10½d.
,, 75 The Scots Guards (Movable Arms) ... ...
,, 74 The Royal Welsh Fusiliers (23rd Regiment) ... 10½d.
,, 33 15th Lancers (Queen's) ... ... 10½d.
,, 17 Somersetshire Light Infantry (Prince Albert's 13th) 10½d.
,, 36 Royal Sussex Regiment ... ... 10½d.
,, 100 The 21st Lancers ... ... 10½d.
,, 8 4th Hussars (Queen's Own) ... ... 10½d.
,, 3 5th Dragoon Guards ... ... 10½d.
,, 98 The King's Royal Rifle Corps ... ... 10½d.
,, 49 The South Australian Lancers ... . 10½d.

No. 124 The Irish Guards ... 10½d. No. 97 The Royal Marine Light Infantry, 10½d.
No. 34 The Grenadier Guards ... 10½d.

No. 122 The Black Watch Highlanders, 10½d. No. 121 The West Surrey Regiment, 10½d.
Copyright models.

No. 104 City Imperial Volunteers ... ... 10½d. box, postage 2d.

No. 30 Drummers and Buglers of the Line ... ... 10½d. Postage
,, 69 Pipers of the Scots Guards ... ... 10½d. 2d.
,, 27 Brass Band of the Line ... ... 1/9, postage 3d.

No. 37 Full Band of the Coldstream Guards ... Price 3/3 Postage 3d.

(Continued on next page.)

A CALL TO ARMS

Pistols for Two

BY W. KEITH NEAL

ROMANCE surrounds the duelling pistol more than any
firearm. It belongs to the days when a man could still
defend his honour without having recourse to a court of
law. It was a private and personal weapon, but it had no small
bearing on the manners and rules of society. Politeness then was
not just a habit; it was a necessity. Those who broke the rules ran
the risk of a challenge which could hardly be refused. One of the
social benefits of pistol-duelling was self-control; and indeed
many of the good manners which have survived to the present
day are the result of chivalry and, on occasion, personal combat.

Pistol-duelling came in during the latter part of the eighteenth
century: it was a fairer method than the sword, as it evened up
the chances. It also had the advantage of being regulated in such
a way that time was given for both parties to think the matter
over. The combat was not one which might be decided on the
spur of the moment by individuals simply drawing swords.
Byron was very much to the point when he wrote:

> It has a strange quick jar upon the ear,
> This cocking of a pistol when you know
> A moment more will bring the sights to bear
> Upon your person twelve yards off or so.

To begin with, duelling with pistols involved the use of any
matched pair of good handling holster pistols, usually the
weapons with which the challenged party was accustomed to
shooting. As the fashion became more established the gun-
makers designed a more specialised weapon, which went
through a series of developments. An example of the first pistols
which could have been used is shown on page 161: a pair of
typical mid-eighteenth-century London-made saddle pistols, by
Israel Segalas, a notable gunsmith of his day. They are well
balanced, with heavy butts bearing a mask, are of smooth bore,
and have no back-sight. They were used instinctively by looking

Opposite: Soldiers with two-handled
swords, from *The Triumph of Maximilian*, 1512

at the target without conscious aiming, rather in the manner of a modern shot-gun. With practice and a certain amount of luck one might just hit a man at twelve yards somewhere in the body. The next step in the evolution of the weapon is shown in the lower illustration on page 161, of a pair of long-barrel pistols with graceful curves to the stock, which is rounded to fit well into the hand. The barrels are eleven and a half inches in length, with silver decoration. There is no back-sight, but a fine double rib running almost the entire length, which does in fact serve the same purpose and makes for quick alignment. These were made by the fashionable Bond Street firm of Griffin & Tow some time in the 1770's. The mounts are still of silver, except for the trigger guard which is blued steel—a wise precaution as this is the part which might catch the eye of an opponent. These pistols are light and beautifully balanced, and were intended for quick instinctive shooting.

At the top of page 162 is shown a pair of true duelling pistols, made by the famous John Twigg of Piccadilly. These represent the earliest form of weapon made specifically for the duel. They were supplied in their mahogany case, complete with all accessories including a separate brass powder measure with which the seconds visually loaded the pistols, so as to leave no doubt that an equal charge went into each weapon. The barrels have changed in form to octagonal for their full length, the two previous pairs having had barrels of an entirely round section. These are clearly made of twist iron, a fashion much in vogue, in which the barrel was forged out of a hammered-out ribbon partly of soft iron and partly of steel, wound round a mandrel and forged and hammered until the joins were welded. When the rod was drawn out the bore was left as a rough tube, which was then fine-bored and polished, the outside being finished with a file and subsequently stained with browning to show the pattern.

These pistols have many interesting features, and, as so often is the case with prototypes, the best of everything went into them. First the stocks: they have squared and flattened sides; this enables the shooter to hold them straight without tipping to one side or the other. They have back- and fore-sights, just

like a rifle, so they can be aimed carefully at a target. The locks
are most ingenious, having an automatically detachable base to
the frizzen which allows the pistol to be fully loaded and primed
with the cock lowered in the safe position. When the pistol is
cocked the frizzen is brought into position and a spring catch
engages the base, so that as the pistol is fired the frizzen opens
the pan and is fired like a normal flintlock. These pistols were
made prior to 1780.

The pair shown at the foot of page 162 are complete in their
case. They have silver mounts dated 1776 and are made by the
famous Wogdon. This maker achieved a reputation second to
none for making duelling pistols; he was in fact the only 'pistol
maker' in London, in that he made these weapons almost to the
exclusion of every other class of weapon. So great was his reputation that an anonymous writer signing himself 'An Irish
Volunteer' published in 1782 'Stanzas on Duelling inscribed to
Wogdon the celebrated pistol maker'. It began:

> Hail Wogdon! Patron of that leaden death
> Which waits alike the bully and the brave.
> As well might art re-call departed breath
> As any sacrifice your victims save.

and continued through various verses such as . . .

> Whilst you survive there's no man's life his own;
> Existence hangs upon a single hair;
> The trigger set, the fatal toss is thrown,
> And all our comfort is in dying fair.

This verse is of interest as it stresses the use of the hair trigger
which was invariably fitted to Wogdon's pistols, and did of
course have to be 'set'. A phrase used in connection with disputes
at this time was: 'It is a Wogdon's case'. This obviously implied
that it was a matter not for lawyers but for a case of Wogdon's
pistols! Of special interest in this illustration is the case in which
this pair of Wogdons is fitted. It is probably the first form cases
took. Made of wood, covered with leather like a miniature
travelling trunk of the period, it is lined inside with wallpaper.

At the foot of page 163 is shown a more sophisticated set of light and elegant pistols, once again by Griffin & Tow. Points of interest are the shorter barrels, careful sighting, and roller bearings on the frizzen springs for quick action.

One of the classic styles of duelling pistol was made with a very curved stock; so curved in fact that it almost resembled a walking-stick handle. The section of the stock was round and finely checkered, and they had beautiful lines. A pair like this is shown at the top of page 163. They were made by Knubley of London. Of the best quality, they are plain except for the barrels, which are of the best imported Damascus and inlaid with silver. These barrels were highly considered, being made of specially figured iron, and they were costly. They enjoyed a considerable vogue, as did also the barrels from Spain.

At the top of page 164 is shown a most handsome set of pistols by the famous maker Henry Walklate Mortimer. Made in his best quality, the barrels are inlaid with gold; they have large gold touch holes and hair triggers. The barrels are smooth-bore but extremely accurate. The author acquired them from a gentleman famous both as an archer and a rifle and pistol shot, the late Ingo Simon. Using a ball, he shot dead, off hand, a starling perched on the roof of his house. The author has practised with these pistols, and, firing at an old milk churn which is approximately the size of the body of a man, he managed to hit and penetrate the churn three times out of five at the range of eighty-five yards. This would be good shooting with a modern revolver, and is only mentioned to show how accurate and formidable a fine duelling pistol can be.

At the foot of page 164 is shown a very elaborate pair of silver-mounted pistols. They are made by Knubley, in his very highest quality, and are most unusual in having such superb decoration. The Parisian maker Le Page and the Versailles maker Boutet both turned out highly decorated duelling pistols, but in England it was rarely done, and these must have been a special order. They handle perfectly, have hair triggers, and are dated on the silver mounts 1791. Also they have a history. They belonged to a well-known English officer who had them during the occupation of Paris after Waterloo. He was challenged to a duel by a Frenchman and elected to use these pistols. In the

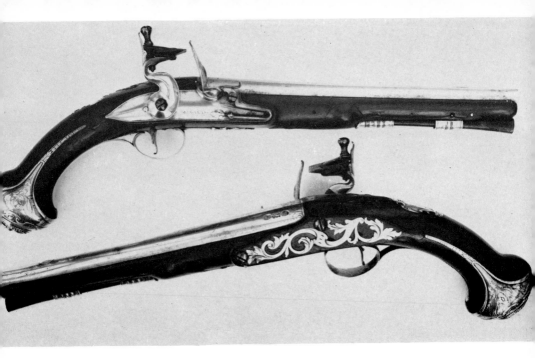

Above: a pair of finely balanced holster pistols with long light barrels, by Segalas, London, c. 1745. They are the true ancestor of the duelling pistol.

Below: the next step in the evolution of the duelling pistol. A pair by Griffin & Tow, London. Note the graceful curved stocks to fit well into the hand for easy alignment. Date about 1770.

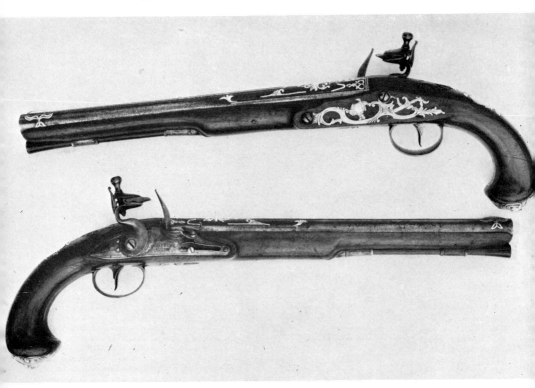

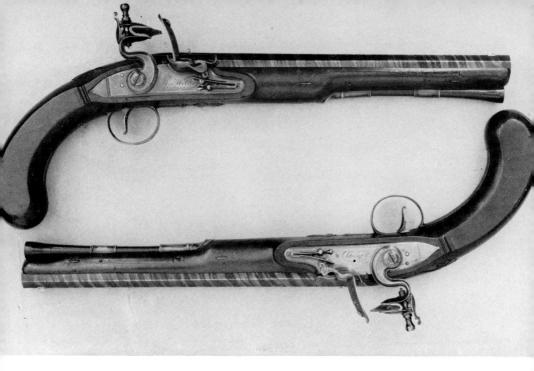

A pair of light duelling pistols by Twigg of London, c. 1775. These are the
early form of the true duelling pistol, with accurate sights, and flat sides to
the grips to help alignment.

Below: the earliest pattern of 'cased set'. Made by Wogdon, the famous
pistol maker, and cased in a leather-covered wooden box, lined with wallpaper. Dated on the silver mounts 1776. Note the first form of wide-cut
checkering on the grips.

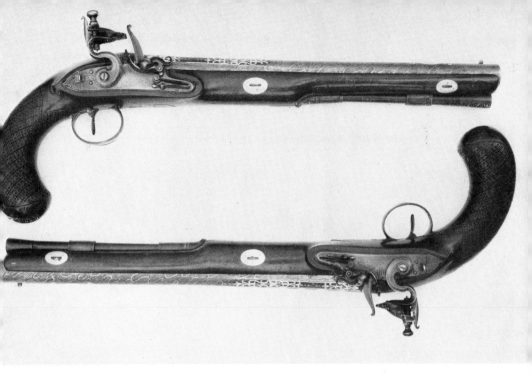

A pair of fine light duelling pistols of about 1790. They have fine imported 'Damascus' barrels and slender curved stocks.

Below: a cased set of light duelling pistols by Griffin & Tow of Bond Street, with elegant lines, careful sighting, and roller bearing in the feather spring Made c. 1780.

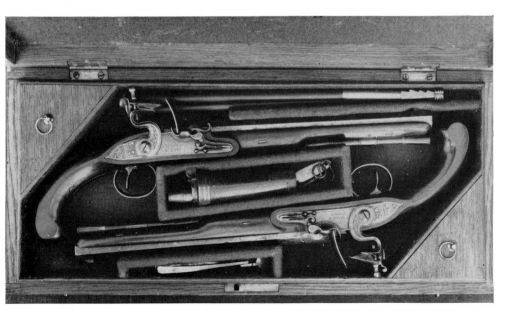

A cased set of best quality Mortimer duelling pistols. The stocks have been shortened to 'half-stock' and the barrels have a rib below to carry the ram-rod. The stock is now finely checkered and the locks have adjustable hair triggers. Made about 1790.

Below: a highly decorated cased pair of duelling pistols. The stocks are in-laid most beautifully with silver scrolls and flowers; they retain their full-length stocks, yet were made later than the preceding pair, in 1791. They are signed Knubley, Charing Cross, London, and are known to have been used in a fatal duel.

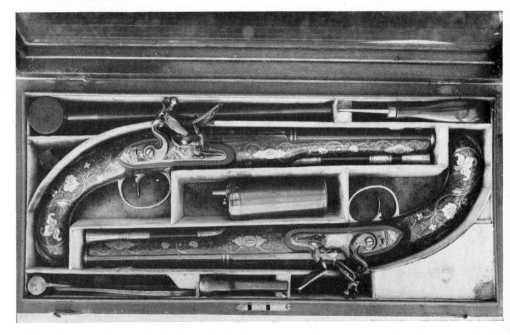

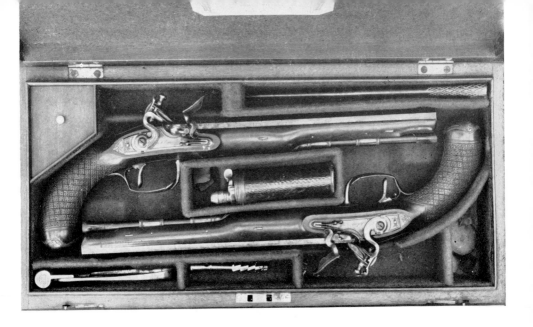

A pair by the famous Durs Egg, marked by his typical checkering of wide cut interspersed with dots. Even the loading rod has a checkered design. Date about 1795.

Below is a pair of saw-handled Mortimer duelling pistols. Note the spur extension to the trigger guard and the spur type of cock copied from the French. The date is about 1800.

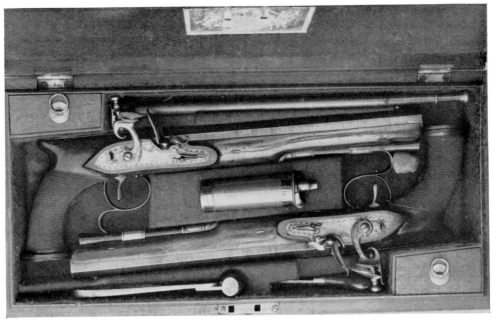

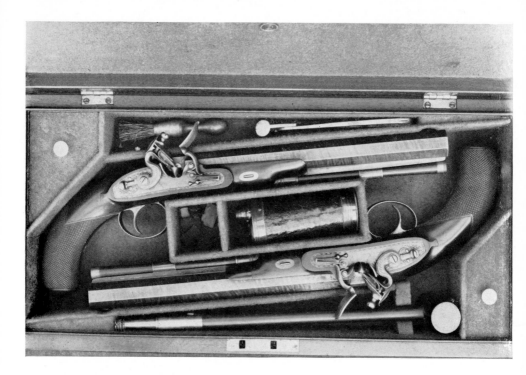

A pair by the famous Joseph Manton, with heavy barrels, scratch-rifled, and superlative workmanship. Date about 1815.

Below: an early pair of copper cap duelling pistols by the noted maker Rigby of Dublin. Saw-handled grips and spur trigger guards, with best damascus pattern barrels. Date about 1825.

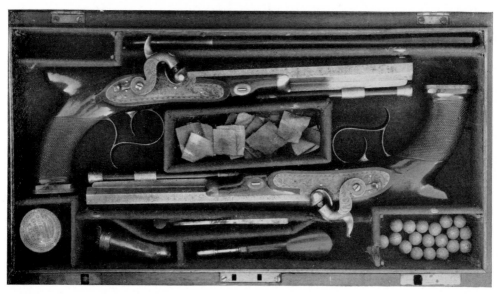

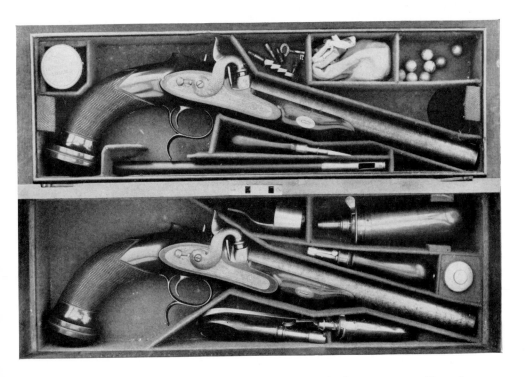

A pair by Samuel & Charles Smith, c. 1830, with the heaviest type of barrel, to give deadly accurate shooting. Fired by a patent form of copper cap known as Smith's Imperial Primer.

Below: a pair by Samuel Nock, of Regent Circus, London. Note the streamlined stocks for fast alignment and the back action locks. c. 1835.

A copper cap duelling pistol by Forsyth made about 1836. Note the complete lack of wooden fore-end and the French style of flat butt.

Below: a Purdey target pistol made on duelling lines. It has a rifled barrel, hair trigger, and no ramrod. The last word in shooting perfection.

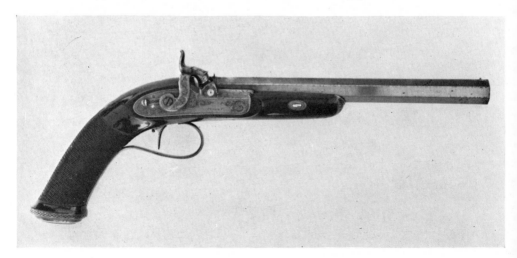

contest the Frenchman was shot dead. They appear to have had almost no use subsequently and remained in the possession of the same family until acquired by the author.

Two of the most famous makers, Durs Egg and Joseph Manton, both turned out splendid examples of duelling pistols; but most of their weapons tended to break away from the elegant light pistol and became heavy-barrel target arms. With these it was possible to make exceedingly accurate shooting at a mark. A Regency buck who could boast of hitting a wafer five times out of ten at twelve paces was not the best man to quarrel with. Practice was put in at the leading London pistol ranges, such as Manton's and Lang's. Bores were often secretly rifled with almost invisible scratch rifling, just enough to give a carefully patched ball enough spin to give super accuracy. A cased set by Joseph Manton are made on these lines, and although heavy to handle compared with the earlier ones there is no doubt they were very deadly in the hands of a calm shooter. Another set by Durs Egg show his individual style: he employed a most attractive form of checkering, cut wide with small dots in the diamond intersections. Egg made many fine pairs of duelling pistols, and they vary to some extent obviously to please the whim of the owner and fit his hand and style of shooting. Joe Manton, on the other hand, seems to have designed a certain pattern of heavy-barrel pistol with half-stock, and hardly varied it at all

As soon as the copper cap superseded the flintlock, makers produced a variety of fine pistols on the new system. Rigby of Dublin was very famous, and a pair of his pistols incorporating the saw-handle grip is shown. He also fitted a spur to the trigger guard which gave better support, especially when the heavier type of arm was used. Rigby introduced the etched and pickled Damascus barrels which are used with the pistols illustrated, and these were renowned for their beauty.

Occasionally a very unusual pair of pistols is encountered, such are those illustrated on page 167. These were made by Samuel & Charles Smith of London, and are of gigantic proportions. They have very heavy round damascus barrels of small bore, the stocks being made for a man with huge hands, and there is no provision for a ramrod. These were probably made entirely as target weapons. They fire Smith's patent Imperial cap, which is a wide shallow primer of his own construction which, he claimed, gave a quicker passage from the flame of the primer to the charge. Even the way these pistols are cased is unusual as they are fitted one below the other in a tray case. The quality is superb. One can only conjecture who the man was for whom they were specially made, but he must have been a giant.

It would be impossible to conclude this summary without referring to two of the greatest makers of English duelling pistols. Forsyth, who invented the percussion system, is now a household name, and long after his original invention the firm continued to make most excellent weapons in the best quality, and always distinctive. A copper cap duelling pistol, illustrated on page 168, shows his inventive design. The stock is in the French style with a flat butt, but shaped well to fit the hand. There is no wooden extension to the fore-end, and the barrel has no bolt in the normal way to secure it in place. It hooks into the false breech but is secured by one square-headed screw, removed in a moment by the same wrench used for the nipple. It is strongly made and almost unbreakable.

Finally we come to a pistol by Purdey. It has perfect lines, with an ebonised stock and a rifled barrel to give the last word in accuracy. There is no ramrod, a separate loading rod being used to serve this purpose and a mallet to drive the ball into the barrel wrapped in its greased patch. These pistols were made more as target weapons than anything else: they fired a very light charge of about three-eighths of a dram of black powder, and would put all their shots into a two-inch target at twenty-five yards off hand. This required great care in the moulding of the bullets; each one had to be perfect and checked for weight, and only those passing the test were used. The barrel was wiped out carefully after each shot, and seldom were more than ten shots fired without completely washing out the barrel. The author possesses a target, shot with a rifled duelling pistol of the same period by Charles Moore. It shows six consecutive shots all cutting each other in the bull. This was achieved by an American at twenty-five yards off hand. Finer shooting than this is impossible, and it was done with an antique pistol made one hundred and fifty years ago.

A Flash of Steel

BY HOWARD L. BLACKMORE

BUDDING psychologist, well primed with Freudian theories, has recently given his opinion that 'the fundamental appeal of the sword to its owner lies in its serving as an embodiment of his phallic energy'. Now I must admit that I have known a number of collectors, small in stature, who seemed to delight in large swords. But really the matter is not as simple as that. For a start, what is the gender of a sword?

She has been the Queen of Weapons, with names like '*Joyeuse*' and '*La Tisona*', for whom men have given their lives. To Kiss the Sword was, and in some places still is, the highest form of oath and homage. The sword was the instrument of royalty. 'Lay on our royal sword your banished hands,' says Richard II. To quote the words of the British coronation ceremony, the sword must 'do justice, stop the growth of iniquity, protect the holy church of God, help and defend widows and orphans, restore the things that are gone to decay, maintain the things that are restored, punish and reform what is amiss, and confirm what is in good order'.

Its touch on the shoulder brought the prize of knighthood. The sword of Arthurian legend was a knight's constant companion, ever ready to leap from its sheath in the cause of weakness and the call of chivalry. A motto often found on a sword blade reads NO ME SAQUES SIN RAISON, NO ME EMBAINES SIN HONOR (Draw me not without reason, sheath me not without honour). The splendid sword of Charles the Bold, Duke of Burgundy, 1467-77, now in the Kunsthistorisches Museum, Vienna, perhaps personifies this ideal more than any other. The hilt and scabbard are of white narwhal horn (thought then to be unicorn), symbolising the purity of the Virgin Mary and Knighthood. The gold mounts bear the emblems of the Order of the Golden Fleece, and the pommel is set with pearls and a great ruby to signify untarnished honour.

The exploits of the *chevaliers d'honneur* and their swords have always stirred poets' imaginations. Here is Tennyson, following closely the words of Malory, on the sword of King Arthur:

There drew he forth the brand Excalibur,
And o'er him, drawing it, the winter moon,
Brightening the skirts of a long cloud, ran forth
And sparkled keen with frost against the hilt:
For all the haft twinkled with diamond sparks,
Myriads of topaz-lights, and jacinth work.

In fact, the knightly fighting sword was rarely set with stones. The one nearest to this description is the sabre or 'pallasch' of the Duke Maximilian I of Bavaria, whose hilt and scabbard are covered with diamonds, topazes, rock crystals and garnets; but it was a dress sword only, part of the Duke's parade garniture.

The fighting sword of the Middle Ages had a plain cruciform hilt of iron with a heavy, double-edged blade capable of terrible cutting strokes. Some of these black-rusted blades have an aura of evil and the smell of death. One thinks of the hilted knife *Hrunting* of Beowolf, whose 'edge was iron stained with poisonous twigs hardened in gore', and Sir Galahad's 'Sword of Strange Hangings', its hilt made from the bones of the serpent Papagast and the fish Ortenians and sheathed in the scabbard called 'Memory of Blood'. The most famous of the legendary makers of swords was Weland the Smith, who, in a trial of skill with another armourer, Amilias, forged a sword called 'Miming'. Its blade was immensely strong and yet so sharp that it cut a bundle of wool floating on water. Amilias, for his part, constructed an armour so much to his own satisfaction that, sitting on a stool, he challenged Weland to try his sword upon him. Weland obeyed, and, there being no obvious effect, asked Amilias if he had felt anything. Amilias replied that it seemed as though iced water had passed through his bowels. Weland then bade him shake himself. Amilias fell dead in two pieces.

It is a good story, often used in other circumstances; but from the evidence of battlefield burials there is every reason to believe that the men using these swords went beserk and cut at each other with maniac force. The historian William of Malmesbury, describing the Siege of Antioch in 1098, tells how

Godfrey of Bouillon, with a Lorrainian sword, cut asunder a Turk who had demanded single combat, so that one half of the man lay panting on the ground while the other half was carried off by the horse at full speed; so firmly did the unbeliever keep his seat. Another also, who attacked him, he clave asunder from the neck to the groin; nor did the dreadful stroke stop there, but cut entirely through the saddle and the backbone of the horse.

On such ugly deeds was the fame of the sword founded. But henceforth no self-respecting owner of an armoury could be without some legendary blade to lend glamour to his collection. A fine sword became a prized gift among princes. Charlemagne, writing to Offa of Mercia, offering him presents for his churches, added, 'and for your own acceptance, I send a bell, a Hungarian sword, and two silk mantles'. Richard Cœur-de-Lion on his way to the Holy Land, receiving rich presents of gold, silver and horses from the King of Sicily, could pay him no greater compliment than to give him in return 'that most excellent sword the Britons call *Caliburn*, and which had been the sword of Arthur, once the valiant King of England'. One of the first great collections of arms and armour, amassed by Charles VIII of France in the Castle of Amboise in 1499, included 'the enchanted sword of Lancelot of the Lake', 'the sword of the giant who was vanquished by the King of France on the Isle of Notre Dame', and a sword called 'La Victoire', the pommel decorated in gold with our Lady on one side and the sun on the other. In 1634 the last sword was being exhibited in the Treasury of the Abbey of St Denis where the monks assured visitors that it was the sword of Joan of Arc.

During the sixteenth and seventeenth centuries the sword underwent many changes. Swords were made for different purposes; for town wear, for riding, for hunting; and the gentleman's fighting sword *par excellence* was now the rapier. This was distinguished by a long narrow blade meant for thrusting, the hand being protected by an elaborate guard. It was no longer a matter of taking a hefty swipe at one's enemy: there were rival schools of fencing to teach a man of honour the complicated movements of arms and legs necessary to manipulate his sword to the position where he could pierce his adversary's equally subtle defence. It was all very wearisome and frightening to the amateur. As George Silver, in his *Paradoxes of Defence* (1599), wrote:

'They in their Rapier-fight stand upon so manie intricate trickes, that in all the course of a man's life it shall be hard to learne them, and if they misse in doing the least of them in their fight, they are in danger of death.'

This was the heyday of the professional swordsman, the braggart and the bully. Tomaso Garsoni, in a book written in 1580, gives a vivid picture of a Venetian bravo of his day, taking a turn up and down the piazza, throwing fierce glances in all directions and slapping his sword loudly on his muscular calves to the spectators' admiring exclamations of 'See! What a piercer of mail! What a cruncher of iron! What a slayer of hundreds!' And what a chaser of women, too: for the pursuit of arms and *amour* so often runs a parallel course. When the trade of weapons in Milan was at its height the Bishop of Agen recorded—without any apparent disapproval—this description of the swordsmen and their companions:

> The ladies receive their attentions with infinite pleasure. For this reason, we all day long see troops of gentlemen of all sorts on splendidly caparisoned mules, on fast slim Turkish horses, on light fleet barbs or spirited genets, on fierce coursers or on quiet hawks, . . . like bees seeking to cull honey from the flowers.

The almost universal adoption of the rapier in Europe brought a great stimulus to the armourer's trade, encouraging the sword-smiths of Solingen, Toledo and Milan to win renown for the quality of their blades. Artists as well began to create decorative designs for hilts of elaborately chiselled steel, inlaid with gold and silver. Swords were now collected as works of art in themselves. The gallery of the great collector Archduke Ferdinand II contained a rapier that must surely be one of the most beautiful of its kind. The blade was by the Milanese swordsmith Antonio Piccinino, but the hilt, probably made in Spain, was of heavy cast gold exquisitely carved and brilliantly enamelled.

Yet always the collector had a liking for *curiosa*, for a sword with a story. In the seventeenth century quite a trade developed in the manufacture of swords with spurious inscriptions such as *Robertus Bruschius Scotorum Rex 1310* (Robert Bruce), *Marchio Rodericus Bivar* (El Cid), *Edwardus Prins Anglie* (the Black Prince). Collectors

have always behaved like infatuated lovers. Convincing them
that the object of their affection is not what it seems is always an
uphill task. They echo the sentiments of Winston Churchill who,
when told that the story of Alfred and the Cakes was false, is
supposed to have growled, 'If it isn't true then it damn well
ought to be.' When that great collector of swords, George IV,
began to assemble his armoury at Carlton House he lost no time
in acquiring the swords of William the Conqueror, the Black
Prince, and Christopher Columbus, found for him with not too
much difficulty by obliging friends and dealers.

George IV may have been ill-advised on historical antiques,
but he was a good judge of swords. A magnificent series of
military swords was made to his own designs by the London
cutlers, many incorporating a famous Spanish, German or
Turkish blade. He was fascinated with Eastern swords, with the
famed blades of watered steel from Damascus and India; and he
bid eagerly for the swords and guns of Tipu Sultan (killed in
1799) which all bore the tiger emblem. Like so many other
collectors, George was carried away by his first enthusiasm and
rapidly overspent his resources. As a result, in 1791, he was forced
to pawn a diamond sword and other trinkets for £25,000.

On the occasion of his state visit to Scotland in 1822 he took a
great fancy to the weapons of that barbaric country whose in-
habitants, so he was told, 'went about almost constantly armed,
partly with a view of being always ready to defend themselves
and partly that being accustomed to the instruments of death
they might be less apprehensive of them'. Inspired by the simple
wish to impress his Scottish subjects and, of course, to bedazzle
the ladies, the King attired himself in full Highland dress and
girded on a magnificent Scottish broadsword and dirk. Somewhat unwisely for a man of his handsome proportions, he wore
a kilt of less than knee length. Poor George! A scurrilous poet
took one look at this mini garment and penned the verses of a
bawdy song which began:

> With his tartan plaid and kelt so wide
> The ladies blush who stand beside
> And as he bows, behind each fan,

Exclaim—Oh! gallant Highlandman
Sing ho, the brawny Highlandman
The handy dandy Highlandman
Oh, happy day, when this way ran
The English-Irish Highlandman.

Then could you see each simp'ring dame
Who blushing to the presence came
To view his face if vain they come
They still may see the Royal Bum . . .

George IV's collection, after his death, was to suffer the fate of
so many others, being broken up and distributed to museums,
institutions and private collections. The main part, however,
remains at Windsor Castle to remind us of a flamboyant yet
pathetic man but a collector in the grand tradition.

Finally we may mention a man of similar tastes if of more
successful application. Alī Dīnār, last Sultan of Darfur, was also
a collector of swords. They were all of the Sudanese pattern
with the heavy double-edged blade and cruciform hilt which
many believe to have been copied from the swords of the
Crusaders. Some of his blades were old, bearing the traces of
swordsmiths' marks and long-forgotten inscriptions, but all were
carefully engraved with his family tree ('Son of Sultan Zakaniya,
son of Sultan Muhammed al-Fadl', etc.). The heavy gold and
silver hilts were treated likewise. Striving always to maintain the
independence of his small country against British intervention,
Alī Dīnār spent his life in the best oriental style, dividing his
time between his army and his harem, the floors of which, we
read, 'under the silvery sand, are impregnated with spices'.
When he was finally killed his collection of swords was broken
up, many being brought home as trophies by British officers,
and it is difficult to judge how many he had. But among his
household accounts was a careful tabulation of his progeny, in
columns of serial numbers, names and sex: over three hundred
of them.

Perhaps there is something in what that psychologist said, after
all.

On the right: a Viking sword from River Witham, at Lincoln *(British Museum)*
On the left: a thirteenth-century sword from River Witham near Lincoln
(British Museum).
In the centre: probably the sword of Henry V, at one time suspended over
his tomb in Westminster Abbey *(Westminster Abbey)*.

Sword of Sancho IV, King of Castile and Léon (1284–95), found beside his mummified body in his tomb in Toledo Cathedral (*Toledo Cathedral*).

Sword, scabbard and belt of Boabdil, last Moorish King of Granada, who died in 1483 after the Battle of Luceno (*Army Museum, Madrid*).

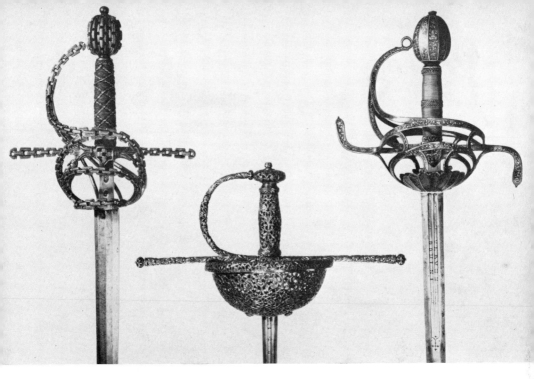

Above: rapier hilts: (left to right)—Italian, *c.* 1590; Spanish, *c.* 1640; English, *c.* 1630 *(Tower of London, Crown Copyright)*.

Below: various hilts: (left to right)—Scottish broadsword, *c.* 1730; French smallsword, *c.* 1750; Italian hanger, *c.* 1680; Dutch 'pillow sword', *c.* 1650 *(Private collections)*.

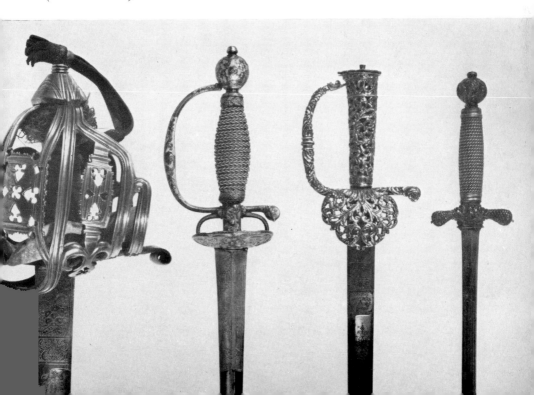

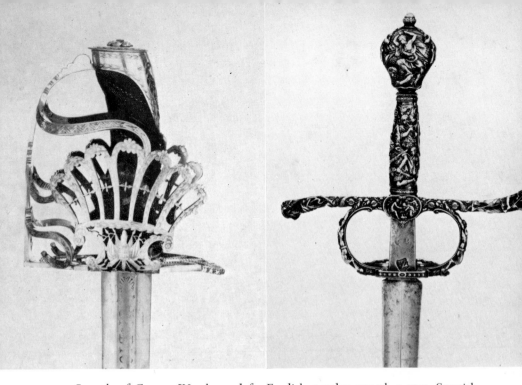

Swords of George IV: above, left: English cavalry sword, *c.* 1800; Spanish blade. Above right: so-called sword of John Hampden; French *c.* 1620; German blade. Below left: Dress sword, French gold hilt set with diamonds, *c.* 1750; remounted with English blade, *c.* 1800. Below, right: Town sword with Italian chiselled-steel hilt, *c.* 1660, presented by Charles XII of Sweden to Duke of Marlborough. *(Royal Collection, Windsor Castle; Crown Copyright.)*

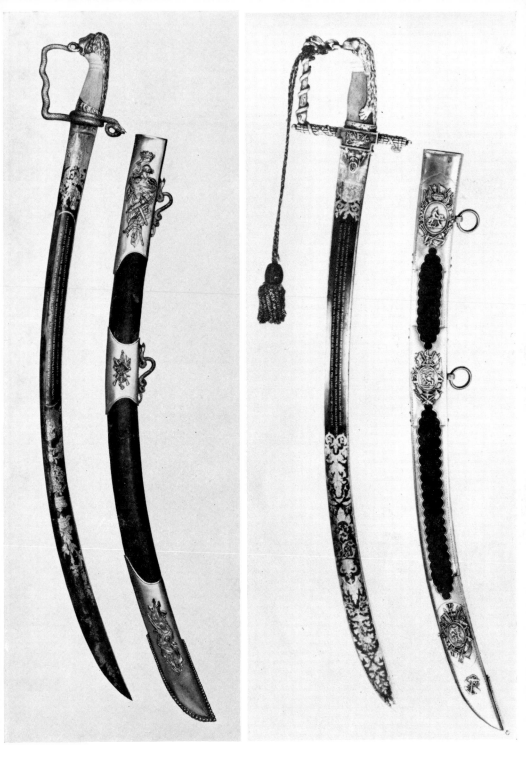

English presentation swords. On the left: to James Cooke, Lt.-Col. of the Trafford House & Hulme Local Militia by his officers. On the right: to Lt Sir William George Parker of H.M.S. *Renommée* for gallant conduct at Viega, 4 May 1806, from Lloyds' Patriotic Fund *(Private collections)*.

A parade sword of Frederick IV of Denmark and Norway, c. 1720;
gilt and enamelled hilt set with pearls (*Rosenborg Castle, Copenhagen*).

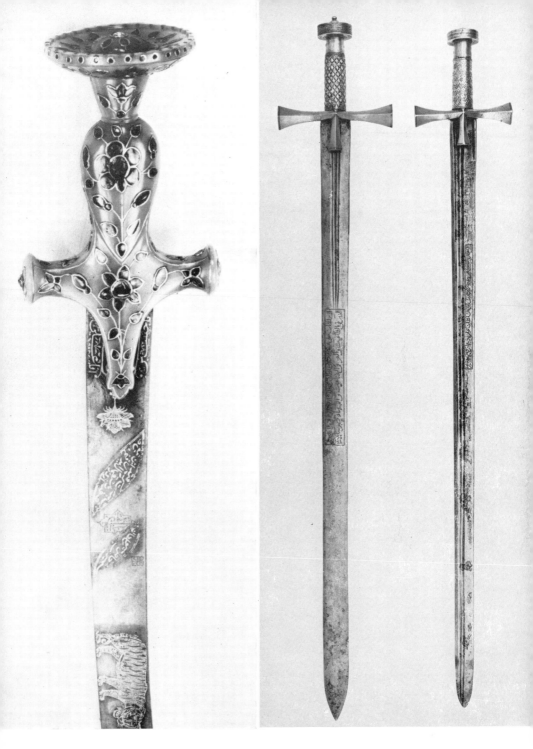

Jade-hilted sword set with precious
stones of Tipu Sultan, killed 1799
(*Wallace Collection*).

Gold- and silver-hilted swords of Alī
Dīnār, last Sultan of Darfur, killed
1916 (*Tower of London, Crown Copyright*).

GRENADIER GUARD
1815

The Bearskins' Silver

BY RONALD LEWIN

PHOTOGRAPHS BY PETER PARKINSON

ONE NIGHT—a night during the spring of 1943—I found myself somewhere in nowhere: an artillery officer supporting a company of the Guards. We were the front line, edging along the side of the African shore. I remember the night mainly because more mosquitoes clustered on my arm than at any other time in my life; but I remember it for another happening. At dawn this company was due to withdraw. There was nothing in sight that seemed human . . . anywhere. But I recall the *timbre* of the voice of that company commander of the Guards giving his instructions to his sergeant-major: 'and, by the way, you *will* see that the men polish their cap badges before we pull out'.

Silver and sergeant-majors have each meant much to the Guards; symbols and traditional performance have been the backbone of the Brigade. Silver—so well presented alongside this article and so lavishly available in the messes of the Guards —has been perhaps disproportionately emphasised as an element in their life. Ouida painted the Brigade as lush, the notion has lingered, and a display of the Grenadiers' silver might over-emphasise the idea. What I wish to say is that the silver on the table, Ouida's image of a whiskery, lackadaisical, effete Victorian

---

The illustrations on the opposite page and on pages 189–91 are of silver models of Grenadier Guards, depicted at different periods in the history of the Regiment, and modelled by Carrington's, of Regent Street, a firm of silversmiths which has specialised since its foundation in 1780 in making presentation pieces for regimental messes. The photograph opposite shows Grenadier Guardsmen of 1889, the year following Kitchener's relief of Khartoum (on the right), and 1815, the year of Waterloo (on the left).

dilettantism, was not true of the Guards battalions in two world wars. It might be observed that in both the officers died because of the tradition represented by the silver: but they also died, in the right part of the battle, because when it came to what Churchill called 'the crunch' the Guards could rise to 'the military necessity'. The silver in these photographs stands for something that might well be represented in gold. And in this achievement the sergeants and sergeant-majors of the Guards—as any member of the Brigade would immediately acknowledge—have been at least a silver streak.

I remember going out on a patrol with a platoon of the Guards during the Mareth Line battle in North Africa; it was commanded by a subaltern thick from the neck up, but gallant as they come; and I remember how he was supported by wary and war-wise sergeants who nursed him through that day... not a gay day. The silver in the mess has always, in the Guards, been supported by the sergeants. The Grenadiers, like their colleagues, acquired the gift which will not let a regiment die—that strange thing which wells from the Colonel to the recruit, a self-confidence. Those sergeants supporting that subaltern in the Mareth Line stood him in good stead. How can one describe to the general public a rare plant, the regimental tradition, which, in the case of the First or Grenadier Regiment of Foot Guards, began with its founding in Flanders by Charles II in 1656—an exiled King surrounding himself with a loyal or Praetorian company of soldiers who would defend him against all comers—its first action was two years later, against Cromwell's troops, at Dunkirk!

One can do so by a chronological narrative, or, as I would prefer, by describing the kind of contemporary event which illustrates the historical continuity comprised, in a sheer physical sense, by the presence of the shining symbols which accompany this text. I know a man who was a regular corporal in the Guards at the time of Dunkirk in 1940—now a distinguished producer in the B.B.C. He got the little body of men for whom he was responsible as far as the coast. There was no boat within reach. He stripped, swam out to some small craft, persuaded his men into it, reached something larger, and voyaged to Dover.

What the Guards had imaginatively done was to send to the various Dunkirk disembarkation points their toughest regimental sergeant-majors to act as reception committees. My naked friend could not parade on the quay-side, so he lolled over the edge of the ship watching his company being lined up by the R.S.M. as they felt their way down the gangways and filtered on to the quay. He said that what was fascinating was to see these men, with their R.S.M. peacocking before them and telling them (in that technical expression the Guards use) how horrible they were, stiffening their backs. He said that they did not wish on their return from Dunkirk to be cosseted by the welfare services: they wished to be treated as men. Somewhere within this story lies the truth of the silver.

The true silver—because it is due to a tradition of loyalty, self-sacrifice, dogged perseverance and a certain ability to link the décor of ceremonial with the realities of modern war that the Grenadiers—and their companion regiments—have retained their place in modern society. If it could be proved that they were simply backward-looking dinosaurs they would be doomed. But it was Ouida's dandies, after all, who with their men served longer in Wellington's Peninsula campaign than anyone else, were a rock at Waterloo, were in every battle of the Crimean War, relieved Khartoum, played a stern part in the South African War, and in 1914–18 won seven V.C.s. To the challenge of 1939–45 the Guards rose in an exceptional way. In France in 1940, and in the Eighth and First Armies in Africa, they performed great deeds, and when the time for re-entry into Europe occurred in 1944 they exhibited an astonishing flexibility, after centuries of striking an infantryman's attitude, by returning to Normandy under Montgomery as the Guards Armoured Division.

This was not surprising. The regiment fought all through Marlborough's B.R.O.M.—Blenheim, Ramillies, Oudenarde, Malplaquet; it fought at Dettingen on the last field where a British monarch, George II, commanded his troops in battle; it was with Sir John Moore in the famous retreat to Corunna; and at Waterloo, because of its shattering of the final assault of the Grenadiers of the Imperial Guard, won the title of Grenadiers.

It knew a good deal about adaptability. Yet to be flexible implies being soft: not so the Grenadiers. The notion of yielding is not theirs. At Inkerman in the Crimean War they held out in the midst of a vicious battle and won four of the first Victoria Crosses ever awarded. A regiment which since 1945 has sent its battalions to Palestine, Malaya, Libya, Egypt, Cyprus, The Cameroons, Guiana, Germany and Northern Ireland has obviously not yielded a jot of its silver tradition. Its motto might well be the old Army phrase, 'It's all according'.

This amounts, I think, to a matter of attitude. The Dunkirk corporal I know matured as a sergeant in the Eighth Army with the Guards Brigade serving there. He was at his company head-quarters one day when it was heavily and precisely shelled. Instinctively he dived under his truck. Then he peered out, as the shells fell, and observed his company commander lying among them in a deck-chair reading *The Times*. Their eyes met. 'Come out, Sergeant,' said the company commander, 'it's much more comfortable out here.' 'And do you know,' my friend said to me, 'I crawled out from underneath the truck, stood to attention, saluted, and said "Yes, sir".' There is a silver thread running directly from that foundation of the regiment by Charles II in 1656 to the much more complex problems it faces with insouciance today.

It has not only been the silver on their tables or the steel in the marrow of their sergeant-majors which has enabled them to maintain this record: it has been a special quality of mind, roughly what the French so realistically call *je m'en foutisme*. Three centuries after 'the Royal Regiment of Guards' was fight-ing at Dunkirk on behalf of Charles II a company of the Guards —but I will not swear it was of the Grenadiers—made its way to the Dunkirk beaches, and successfully embarked and sailed across the Channel. As they came off their ship a journalist went up to the company commander, the major who, it might be said, had led them from a sort of Hell to a sort of Paradise. He asked the major what it was like on the other side of the water. 'My *dear*!' the major replied, 'the *noise*! And the *people*!'

Silver, or gold—or what?

Soldiers of the First Regiment of Foot Guards of 1745 (on the right) and 1792. In 1743 the Regiment played an important part in the defeat of the French at Dettingen—the last occasion on which an English king, George II, commanded his troops in battle.

Grenadier Guardsman in uniform that would date him between 1857 and 1870. The double-breasted tunic worn during the Crimean War went out in 1857 and was replaced by the single-breasted type shown here. The figure is wearing the Crimea Medal, 1854–6, with the four clasps that were awarded, one for each major battle of the war.

Grenadier
Guardsman of
the Independent
Parachute
Company
formed in 1948.

Dressed to Kill

BY JAMES LAVER

IF THE FEMALE is a breeding specialisation, the male (the biologists tell us) is a fighting specialisation. This may seem a shocking statement to modern high-minded pacifists, but the history of the human race would seem to bear it out. The story of human advance is the story of the increasing sophistication of weapons. This is the one department of technology which never shows a decline.

The one reason why *homo sapiens* was able to steal a march on other animals was the discovery that he could supplement his nails and teeth (never in his case very effective) with artificial aids. A stone in the hand was more damaging to an enemy than the hand itself, even when clenched in a fist, could ever be. The next stage was the discovery that the stone could be *thrown*, and this began the long struggle between the projectile and the protection against it, which is still with us as a modern problem. From time to time defensive devices gain on offensive weapons. One has only to think of the stalemate of World War I. Then came the tank, and the battlefield was fluid once more.

One of the most astonishing effects of the device to provide as much protection to the fighting man as possible was the development of armour. It began as a mere series of metal discs or plaques sewn on to a leather jerkin. Chain mail was a marvellous invention as, although heavy, it did not hamper movement very much. A breastplate and a helmet were obvious additions, and the evolution continued until the whole body was enclosed in

Opposite: Gothic war-harness for man and horse, probably by Matthis Deutsch of Landshut, South Germany, c. 1480 (Wallace Collection, London). This period was the high-water mark of effective plate armour for use in battle. A knight so equipped was almost invulnerable unless he could be unhorsed, when he found it very difficult to rise from the ground and was at the mercy of any foot soldier provided with a thin-bladed dagger which could be inserted in the joints of the armour.

plate armour. This required immense skill on the part of the armourers until in the fifteenth century the whole process was complete. The warrior—or rather the knight, the aristocrat—had become a lobster, enclosed in a hard shell and, in theory at least, invulnerable. The high-water mark was reached when the incredible craftsmanship of the Augsburg armourers and others like them produced the so-called 'Gothic' armour of the last quarter of the fifteenth century.

It is at this time that we have chosen to begin our study. But meanwhile woman had been developing her own weapons. What we call 'Fashion' had only been invented about a century before. Previously, for a thousand years or so after the fall of the Roman Empire, women had been wrapped up like parcels, their hair concealed by a veil, most of the face concealed by a wimple, and the whole body wrapped in voluminous and shapeless garments which concealed the natural lines of the female body.

And then, suddenly, in a single generation, the whole thing began to move. In the luxurious courts of France and Burgundy, towards the end of the fourteenth century, Fashion was invented. Isabeau of Bavaria might be called the first 'leader of Fashion'. And the 'weapons of Fashion' were three: tight-lacing, décolletage and elaborate head-dresses. The last of these was sternly denounced by the moralists of the period, and not, perhaps, without reason. For what the Devil, or those inspired by him, had discovered was that the veil, hitherto the very symbol of female modesty, could be used not to conceal the face but to draw attention to it. It could be raised above the head by frames or wires, it could be stiffened or made transparent, and the culmination of this perversion of the original purpose of the veil can be seen in the 'butterfly' head-dresses of about 1480. Brasses of the period show this very clearly, as well as the nipped-in waist and the quite startling décolletage.

In the opening years of the sixteenth century the great days of armour were over. The armourers were even more skilful than before, but they now began to indulge in fantasy. Armour was no longer designed with a view only to its efficiency; it began to ape the fashions of the day, and to echo its pinkings and slashings. It also began the curious process by which it shrivelled, so to speak, from the feet upwards, a process which, by the middle of the seventeenth century, left only a breastplate. In the eighteenth century this shrank still further until only the symbolic gorget was left.

The early sixteenth century which saw the beginning of the end for armour also witnessed the first military uniforms in the modern sense. It is indeed the disappearance of armour which makes 'uniform' possible. The medieval knights, however much their accoutrements resembled one another, strove for as much *difference* as possible by means of crests and coats-of-arms, many of which have survived as proud heraldic distinctions. The ordinary people when gathered into armies did not wear any special costume, unless they were the personal retainers of some great noble, in which case they wore a distinguishing badge or livery, and it is probable that this livery is the origin of the military uniforms of ordinary soldiers.

It is thought that the first time English troops were clothed by the Government (but this was, for long, quite exceptional) was in the reign of Edward III who raised a thousand men in Wales, armed them with pikes and provided for each a mantle and a tunic. In 1485 Henry VII raised the body known as the Yeomen Warders of the Tower of London. They were reorganised by Henry VIII who gave them the costume which, with the addition of an Elizabethan ruff, they still retain. This and the costume of the Papal Guards, at the Vatican, are the two oldest uniforms extant.

Of course, 'dressing up to fight' was no new thing, indeed it goes back to the Night of Time, even if for the primitive savage it was not a matter of putting on clothes but of painting the skin, putting on war-paint, as the phrase still has it. The idea was to make the appearance, especially of the face, as frightening as possible. This desire to terrify the enemy only survived into modern times in such vestigial forms as the death's head on the hussars' headgear and the bare ribs of the skeletons painted on the warrior's body and later transformed into the froggings of his tunic.

This desire to terrify the enemy is only one of the six aims of military uniforms. Another is to protect the wearer which, as

Engraving from *The Exercise of Arms for Calivres,
Muskettes and Pikes*, by Jacob de Gheyn, 1607

we have seen, reached its highest point in late medieval armour. Unfortunately it hampered the wearer's movements to such an extent that an unhorsed knight found it difficult to rise from the ground without help. A third motive is to distinguish friend from foe, but this end can sometimes be attained by merely wearing a scarf or badge. A fourth is to establish in plainly visible form the hierarchy of rank; a fifth is to reinforce the feeling of solidarity and *esprit de corps*; and a sixth is to enhance the manly pride of the wearer. These aims have not all been manifested to the same degree in different epochs, and some are plainly incompatible with one another.

To enhance a soldier's manly pride is partly obtained by making him hold his head up—hence the tight collar or neckband so often seen in the uniforms of the past and this even at the cost of reducing the fighting man's efficiency. Another way to enhance his manly pride is to make him feel *bigger*: by putting a stripe down his leg to make it seem longer (it is interesting to note that this device was already in use in the sixteenth century); to broaden his shoulders with epaulettes; and, most important of all, to increase the height of his hat.

Nothing is more striking in the history of military uniform than the way in which any headgear given to a soldier seems to *grow*. An obvious example is the 'bearskin' of the Guards, which was originally no more than the fur edging of his cap. Even when the headgear does not lend itself to elongation the same effect is produced by a large upright plume. All these devices make a soldier feel 'more of a man', and there can be little doubt that the girls agree with him, or did so in the days when uniform did not merely mean battledress. For in modern war costume the Utility Principle has, of necessity, triumphed over both Panache and Sex Appeal, the final term being reached in camouflage—that is, the desire to be invisible.

That was the last thing the soldier of former days desired, and that was the last thing the girl who 'walked out' with him desired, for the envious eyes of other girls regarded the soldier-escort as 'every inch a man' with, as we have noted, a few extra inches added by the military tailors, with all the masculine characteristics emphasised and exaggerated.

But the exaggeration of sexual characteristics has always been the underlying motive of female costume, and since men tended to choose their partners in life by their attractiveness as women, the problem was to keep their interest alive by displaying one 'charm' after another. This is what is at the back of that changing emphasis which we call Fashion, and the fundamental principle behind it is the strange phenomenon known to psychologists as the 'Shifting Erogenous Zone'.

We have already noted that in the late fourteenth century the three weapons of Fashion were invented together in the course of a single generation. But these three—*décolletage*, tight-lacing and striking headgear—are not Fashion's only weapons. Almost any part of the female anatomy has been made to serve its term, so that in one epoch wide hips have been admired, in another legs, and in another the back. In the year 1930 we could see the transition from legs to back happening before our eyes.

There is, however, one significant difference between most of the fashions of the past and those of the present. Just as Panache has vanished from the soldier's uniform, so has its feminine equivalent vanished from women's dress. A girl in the recent mini-skirt might be seductive enough, but she could hardly be said to be 'dressed to kill'. We have only to think of Queen Elizabeth with her farthingale, her bodice sewn all over with jewels, her divided ruff (thereby getting the advantage of *décolletage* also), or of Marie-Antoinette with her embroidered, paniered skirt, her froth of lace at the elbows, her high, powdered head; we have only to think of the Empress Eugénie with her immense crinoline, her skirt with a thousand yards of tulle sewn round and round in flounces. We have only to think of the *dame du monde* (or still better the *dame du demi-monde* of the Belle Époque) to see that even the fashionable woman of today cuts a poor figure in comparison. Here is a description of an evening dress of 1899:

A gored skirt of pale yellow silk lined with sateen, three shaped flounces of white tulle, the edge of each with narrow moiré ribbon run on. The top flounce slopes up from a narrow point in front. Bodice, laced behind, is covered with white chiffon full all round, with double pleatings round the square cut top. A double waterfall of chiffon descends on the left side. Silk shoulder straps with bunches of roses; yellow chine silk sash.

Day dresses were hardly less elaborate. We hear, in 1901, of a

> Teagown in rose-pink accordion-pleated nun's veiling and ecru lace.
> Tucked sailor collar surrounded with guipure. Soft knitted sash of cream
> crêpe de chine surrounds the figure and trails to the foot. Bishop sleeves,
> with tight band at the elbow and expanding into angel sleeves, edged with
> lace. Lace flounce to the hem of skirt.

Even more astonishing than the combination of 'bishop' and
'angel' sleeves is the price of this confection: four guineas. One
can only wonder how much even of that modest sum was paid
to the seamstress who actually stitched the dress. On the other
hand it was possible to pay £200 for an embroidered evening
gown.

The coronation of King Edward VII, says Dr Willett Cunning-
ton, 'encouraged fashions to take more expensive forms, on the
plea that extravagance was both loyal and good for trade'. It was
what has been called 'the last Good Time of the Upper Classes',
for the dresses seemed exclusively designed for those who spent
their time in England at garden parties or Ascot and, the moment summer was over, followed the swallows winging south
to Beaulieu and 'Monte'. 'The dressmaker's art', we are told by
a contemporary commentator, 'is very rapidly reaching the top-
most pinnacle of perfection. . . . Dress grows more perplexing
and bewildering every season.' The motive was frankly stated:
the modes of the moment were labelled 'this Season's Seduc-
tions' and we read of a 'temptatious teagown which absolutely
defines the figure in a manner which is insinuating'.

The modern girl is no more likely to possess a teagown than
an Elizabethan farthingale. Everything has been stripped to the
bone—or should we say the midriff! Modern modes no doubt
have their own seduction but they rely on other and simpler
means.

As for man! Where are the exquisitely polished silk hats, the
highly polished boots (even the bootlaces *ironed* every morning
by one of the maids), the frock-coats, the immaculate linen at
wrist and throat, stiffly starched in order to make any active
pursuit—or work—impossible? Even soldiers have lost all the
panache they once exploited, and modern military garb is no

more a 'uniform', in the old sense, than the dungarees of factory hands. A few years ago there was a curious vogue for buying old military uniforms and sporting them in King's Road, Chelsea. But those who sported them would certainly not have appealed to any sergeant-major in history. Clothes are still used, presumably, to attract the opposite sex, but neither men nor women in the modern age could claim that they are 'dressed to kill'.

Opposite is illustrated armour for foot-combat, made at Greenwich, c. 1530, for King Henry VIII (Tower of London Armouries, *Crown Copyright*). Armour had been made in England since the fourteenth century, but in the early sixteenth century the best armourers in Europe were acknowledged to be those of Augsburg, Nuremberg and Milan. Henry VIII, impressed by a suit of armour sent to him by the Emperor Maximilian I, brought over some 'Almain' armourers to improve the quality of the work done at Greenwich. The suit shown is one of the earliest produced there. As it was intended for fighting on foot, the rump also is protected. Note the 'duckbill' shoes and a codpiece of dimensions appropriate to the appetites of the royal wearer.

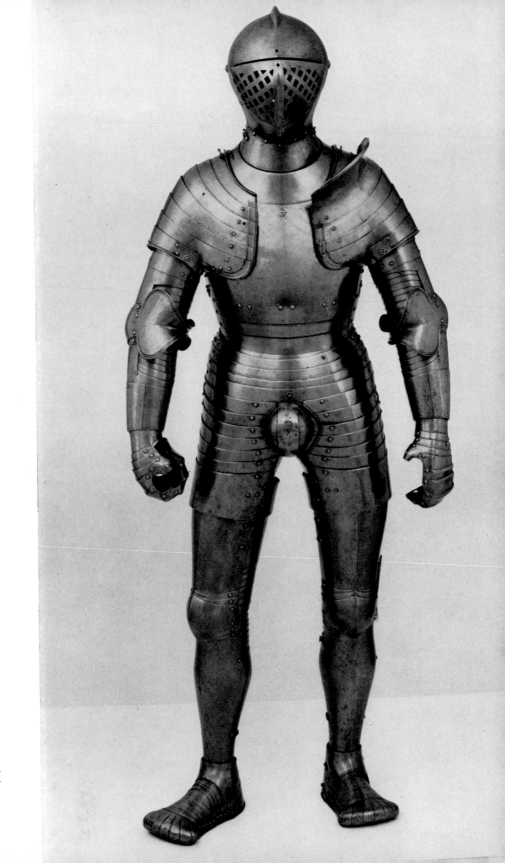

201

Above is a portrait supposedly of Lucrezia Borgia (1480–1519) by Bartolomeo Veneziano, in the Frankfurt Art Gallery. She is dressed (or undressed) as Flora, and was presumably taking part in one of the mythological pageants so popular at the Courts of Renaissance princes, even if the prince in question was actually the Pope.

Opposite is armour by Kolman Helmschmied of Augsburg, c. 1530 (Kunsthistorisches Museum, Vienna). In the early sixteenth century the functional aspect of armour was beginning to be superseded by extravagant suits echoing the civilian dress of the period, even to the puffings and slashings which must have taxed the skill even of the armourers of Augsburg. Protection in battle had given place to the desire to make an effect in a ceremonial parade.

Armour for horse and man made for Otto Heinrich, Count Palatine of the Rhine (1502–1559), by Hans Ringler of Nuremberg, dated 1532 and 1536 (Wallace Collection). The breastplate is decorated with the figure of the Virgin and Child in glory. The total weight of the armour was 61½ lb.

Opposite: 'The Judgement of Paris,' by Lucas Cranach, c.1530 (Royal Museum of Fine Arts, Copenhagen).

Above is a portrait of Mary Fitton, thought to be Shakespeare's 'Dark Lady of the Sonnets', by John Bettes II (in the collection of F. H. M. FitzRoy Newdegate, Esq.), showing Elizabethan 'fashion' in all its ornate elaboration.

Opposite is the armour of Robert Dudley, Earl of Leicester, made by John Kelte, c. 1565 (Tower of London Armouries, *Crown Copyright*). It was for tilting, not for battle, and is described in an inventory of 1611 as 'one Tylte armoure compleate graven with the ragged staff', the Earl's device.

The dress of the unknown girl above, painted in 1569 by an anonymous artist (Tate Gallery), is in marked contrast to the dress worn by Mary Fitton, but even more laden in jewels. The miniature portrait by Nicholas Hilliard, opposite, c. 1590, is of George Clifford, 3rd Earl of Cumberland (National Maritime Museum, Greenwich). The Earl became 'Queen's Champion at the Tilt' in 1590, and on Ascension Day of that year appeared as 'Knight of Pendragon Castle' surrounded by figures from Arthurian romance. He is shown in the act of challenging, with his gauntlet flung down, and he wears an elaborate allegorical costume: an embroidered surcoat and armour studded with stars. The Queen's glove is pinned to the front of his helmet. Tilting at this period had dwindled to a pageant.

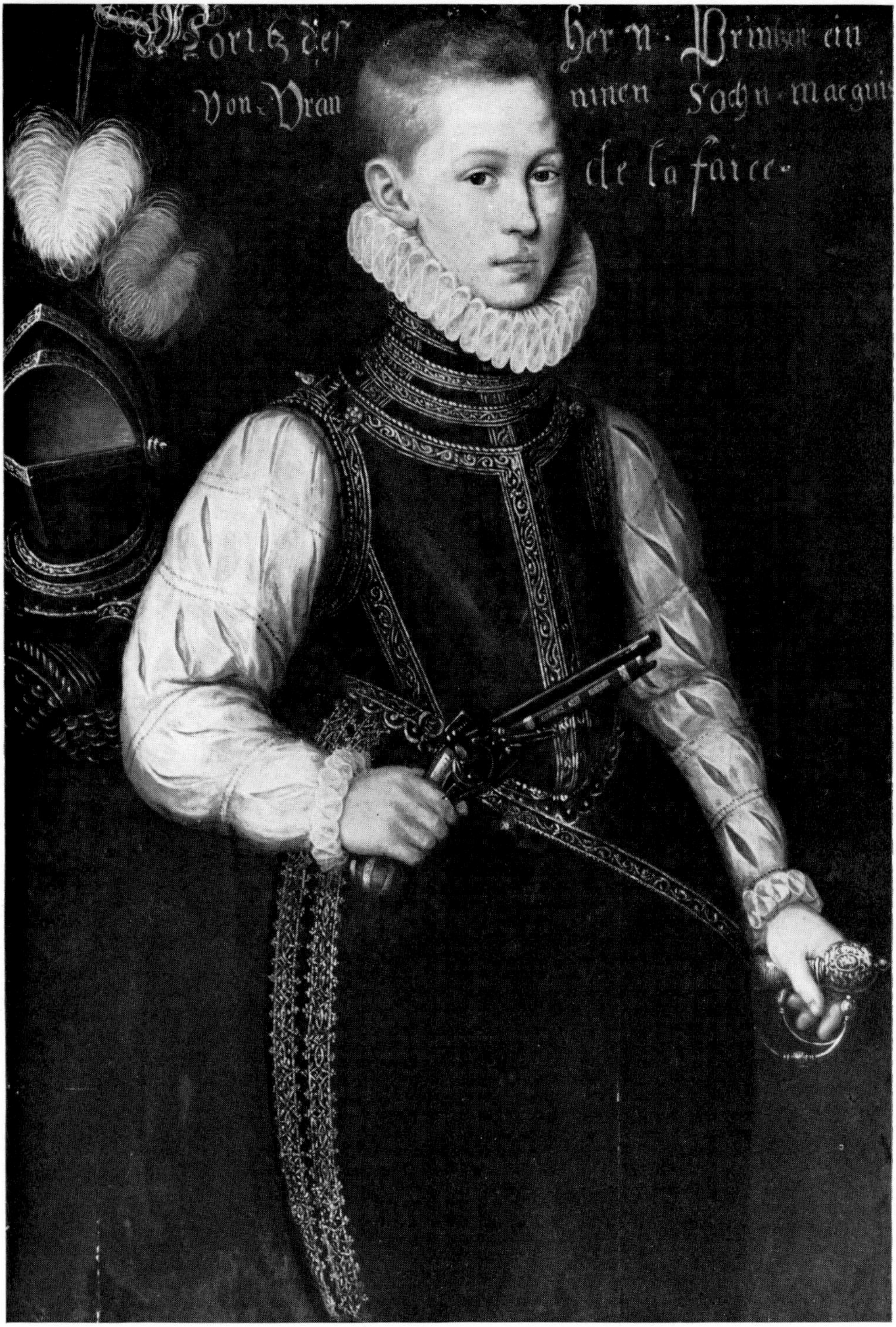

In the seventeenth century even children were 'dressed to kill'. Opposite is Maurice, Count of Nassau, at the age of fourteen (painting by an anonymous artist in the collection of H.M. the Queen of the Netherlands). He is wearing a breast plate, armour having by this time shrunk away, as it were, from the lower limbs. The little girl's portrait above, known as '*The Princess*', was painted by Paulus Moreelse (1571–1638) and is now in the Rijksmuseum, Amsterdam. Children at this period were dressed in costumes almost identical with those of their elders.

The Duke of Marlborough, a drawing by Michael Dahl in the British Museum. He is shown in armour, but this is merely the convention of the time in depicting soldiers. The plumed helmet is an added absurdity, as it would have been impossible to put it on while wearing a full-bottomed wig.

Frances Pierrepont, Countess of Mar, c. 1723 (from the portrait by Kneller in the collection of the Earl of Mar and Kellie). An interesting example of the way in which women, when they adopt masculine pursuits, masculinise the *upper part* of their costume only.

Eighteenth-century styles. Above, Madame Adélaide, 1778, by Adélaide Labille-Guiard (1749–1803), known as the 'peintre des Madames', i.e. the princesses of the Royal House (Phoenix Art Gallery, Arizona). Opposite is a portrait by Thomas Gainsborough of an officer of the 4th Regiment of Foot, c. 1775 (National Gallery of Victoria). His 'armour' has now shrunk to a crescent-shaped 'gourget' hung round the neck.

The Earl of Uxbridge at Waterloo, an anonymous contemporary engraving. The hussar uniform is a striking example of the curious phenomenon of 'fossilised' costume. Hungarian mercenaries were employed as light cavalry in the armies of Louis XIV. They wore their national costume with the frogged tunic and the short fur-trimmed jacket attached to one shoulder. By the end of the eighteenth century this costume, smartened and bedizened, was worn by hussar regiments in all the armies of Europe.

A fashion plate from Heideloff's *Gallery of Fashion*, 1797. Perhaps we cannot do better than quote the original description: 'Hyde Park, Riding Dress. The front hair combed plain: the sides and hind hair in ringlets. Black beaver hat, with a gold band and tassels; round blue ostrich feather placed in the front of the hat. Riding Dress of blue cloth. Double plaiting of *Valenciennes* lace round the neck. Large gold hoop ear-rings. York tan gloves. Purple Spanish leather shoes.' An example of male influence on female costume.

Above and opposite are portraits of Lady Cardigan, by Richard Buckner, and the seventh Earl of Cardigan, the 'Hero of Balaclava', by A. F. de Prades (both reproduced by courtesy of Edmund Brudenell, Esq.). The aptly named Miss Adeline Horsey de Horsey was a famous *equestrienne* who shocked her contemporaries by riding in Rotten Row without a groom, and even more by openly becoming the mistress of Lord Cardigan. After the death of his first wife he married her, he being sixty and she thirty-three. They lived in great state at Deene Park but the Queen disapproved and the 'County' refused to call.

In her old age Lady Cardigan had her revenge by publishing her
memoirs, full of scandalous details of aristocratic life. She died in
1915, aged ninety-one. The frontispiece of the present book shows her
in riding costume on her chestnut hunter. Lord Cardigan is here
shown in the uniform of the 11th Hussars, on his favourite charger.

In the late 1960's a number of young men and women took to wearing second-hand uniforms. In the photograph opposite, taken by Colin Jones for *The Observer*, they are seen watching a parade of real soldiers: the Life Guards on the Mall. Contrast their self-consciousness with the elegant assurance of the young Queen Victoria, portrayed above in a lithograph for *The Fly*, August 10, 1839, as she leaves Windsor to review her troops, accompanied by the Duke of Wellington and the King of the Belgians.

Venus and Mars in nineteenth-century guises. The lithograph by T. C.
Wilson above represents early Victorian sentiment at its most lush, with
male and female in full-dress uniform. By the end of the century, after
many years of peace, the trappings of war had given place to the uniform of
the grouse moor, the musket to the shot-gun, the charger to the spaniel.
The drawing by S. Begg opposite, which appeared in *Black and White* in 1890,
shows a gentleman dressed to kill (a bird, not a foe), though the lady is
intent upon her traditional target.

223

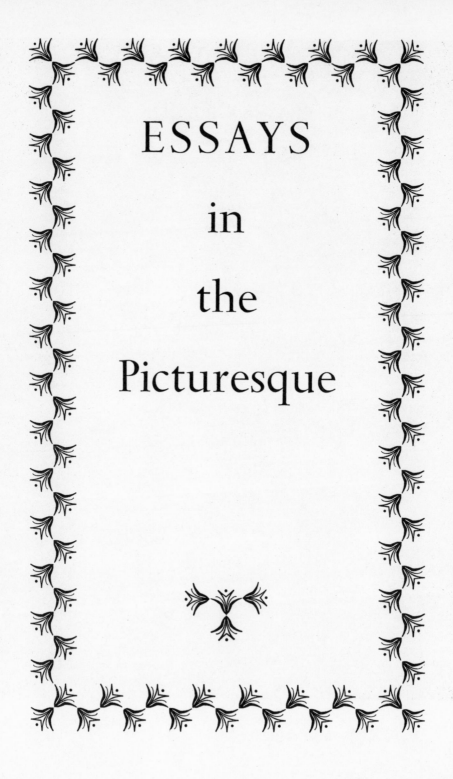

ESSAYS

in

the

Picturesque

Horsley Towers

BY ROBERT TYRRELL

PHOTOGRAPHS BY MARIA TYRRELL

HAVING survived the shock of seeing Horsley Towers for the first time one would never suspect that this flamboyant jumble of buildings had any link with the poet, aesthete and lover of Greece, George Gordon, Lord Byron. Yet the connection is a close family one, for Byron's daughter, Ada Augusta, was the first wife of the Lord Lovelace whose architectural imagination ran riot in this pretty Surrey village, to produce a folly which compares with any in the British Isles.

But the story began somewhat differently. Between 1820 and 1829 Sir Charles Barry, architect of the Houses of Parliament, built here a house in the Elizabethan style for a private client. A few years later, in 1837, it was purchased by William, 8th Lord King, who was created 1st Earl of Lovelace in Queen Victoria's coronation year. Born in the year of Trafalgar, the Earl was a truly unusual man. Not only was he an architect, civil engineer and Fellow of the Royal Society, but he also became in later life a magistrate for Surrey, Honorary Colonel of the 3rd Surrey Militia, and Lord Lieutenant of the county. Local records of the time describe him as '. . . a considerable classic scholar and a man of great scientific attainments'.

To say that the Earl led a full life is an understatement. When young, he entered the Diplomatic Service, and he learned fluent modern Greek while acting as secretary to Governor Lord Nugent in the Ionian Islands. He also travelled widely in Egypt and Arabia and he personally knew Mehemet Ali, founder of the last Egyptian dynasty. In addition to this he won the Telford Silver Medal for his paper on 'Harbours of Refuge', read before the Institution of Civil Engineers, who made him an honorary member. The French Society of Civil Engineers granted him a diploma. Others of his interests included climatology, meteorology, agriculture, forestry and, according to local sources, 'quiet rides on a favourite little pony'.

Once established at Horsley, Lord Lovelace set to work making alterations and additions to the property, personally supervising all the works. He built '. . . the elaborate towers, with their water storage tanks supplied from an artesian well 800 feet deep; the cloisters; the house chapel and many other features'. A local history cites the materials used as being 'red, black and white bricks and picked flints'. However, there is no architectural term that expresses the staggering results. There does not seem to have been any overall plan in the designer's agile brain. Towers, terraces and galleries seem to have been put down regardless, like a child playing with toy bricks.

Amongst other talents the new owner was also an expert in the craft of bending wood by using steam, and one of the roof-trusses in the dining hall is inscribed to record that the process was used during its construction in 1847.

One of the most interesting buildings is the chapel, which is tucked away behind a tower and hemmed in by walls—a most unusual situation. On a sunny day the inside gives a bewildering impression of colour as all the windows are of variegated stained glass whilst the floor and walls are set with Minton tiles. The effect is kaleidoscopic but hardly conducive to quiet meditation. His lordship's passion for towers is obvious from the photographs, and, had his home ever been besieged, it is certain that the defenders would have had a great advantage. The walls are very thick, and most of the windows very small; local people used to say the reason for this was to prevent anyone looking out of them to watch the Earl ride past.

But of all the strange features at Horsley Towers the 'Tradesmen's Tunnel' is surely the most bizarre. The house was originally approached by no less than four carriage drives, but the Earl built a special entrance so that tradesmen could reach the house without being seen or heard. This comprises a brick tunnel some hundred yards long, with twin bores for part of its length near the inner portal. It gives access to what were the kitchen quarters, so that the butcher, the baker and the milkman were kept discreetly out of sight. (One cannot help being reminded of the tunnel built at Welbeck Abbey by the 5th Duke of Portland, a mile and a quarter long, and big enough to take a horse and carriage.) Over the years so much of the estate has been sold for building that the other drives are no longer in use, and Horsley Towers can now only be reached through the tunnel, which must make it unique.

The Earl's erections contrast oddly with the classic lines of Sir Charles Barry's 'Elizabethan' mansion. However, any suspicion that Lovelace might have got his grotesque inspirations from the claret bottle or from dreams induced by over-rich eating are dispelled by a sentence in his obituary which says he was '. . . a vegetarian and altogether eschewed the use of tobacco and alcoholic beverages'.

If the Earl and his demesne were extraordinary, his bride was a match for them both. Ada Augusta Byron, born in the year of Waterloo, was one of the most intelligent ladies of her day. She was described as 'a handsome, delicate, eccentric young woman', and she had inherited her mother's talent for mathematics. So brilliant was Ada at this (then) unladylike branch of learning that she became an intimate friend of Charles Babbage (1792–1871), who was one of the pioneers of the calculating machine, and she even wrote a book on his work in this field. We may well imagine that, if the conversation ever languished, Ada was always ready to swap quadratic equations across the dinner table or ask some jolly little riddle about the square root of minus one!

Despite her husband's ascetic habits she invented a betting system for racing, but this had only a limited success, for, as a biographer put it, 'it would have been infallible had it not been for the interference of horses and jockeys'. Ada was also an excellent pianist, but she is said to have affected a high-handed and self-conscious manner because she always felt she was an object of curiosity on account of her father's licentious behaviour. This is hardly surprising, for his portrait at home had always been veiled by a green curtain, and she was brought up to believe that he was an ogre. Moreover, Ada's mother was a difficult character and showed a curiously two-faced attitude towards her daughter. Lady Byron was on the most friendly terms with her son-in-law and often discussed intimate family matters with him behind Ada's back. In all the circumstances it is surprising that the poet's only child emerged as such a clever and talented person, and it was probably a good thing that she virtually never knew her father.

The Earl of Lovelace died in 1893 at the age of eighty-eight, having survived Ada Augusta by forty-six years, during which time he married again. They had had three children, including a male heir, and the house stayed in the family for a time; but in 1919 the third Earl sold it to T. O. M. Sopwith, the celebrated aircraft engineer and yachtsman. Only a year later Horsley Towers was again on the market and, although much of the 2,000-acre estate was disposed of, the house remained empty until 1926 when it became a girls' school named St Michael's. A note in the prospectus mentions that cricket was played and that the lake was used for boating and bathing. Parents were warned, however, that 'No hampers are allowed, but cakes for birthdays and wholesome sweets in moderation may be sent from home'.

In 1939 Horsley Towers was bought by the Central Electricity Authority, and it is now used as a Training Establishment by the Electricity Council which runs courses on all aspects of this vital industry. We may be sure that two such scientifically minded people as the 1st Earl and Countess of Lovelace would have approved of the new rôle of their old home; but what Lord Byron, so deeply versed in the beauties of ancient Greece, would have thought about the architecture can hardly be imagined.

Opposite: one of the towers which Lord Lovelace added to the Victorian-Tudor house built by Barry, of which part of the original façade may be seen on the left.

Above: a view of Horsley Towers across the moat. The double tower houses a water supply drawn from an artesian well eight hundred feet deep. The chapel roof can be seen behind the wall on the right of the photograph.

At the top of the opposite page may be seen the twin tunnels giving access to the servants' quarters—the only entrance now in use. Below, like an illustration to Grimm's Fairy Tales, is the gate lodge to one of the original carriage drives, now disused.

The Victorian Garden

BY MILES HADFIELD

IN MY well-used 1897 edition of *The English Flower Garden* William Robinson wrote of the type of gardening then largely prevalent: 'We cannot have the foregrounds of beautiful English scenery daubed with a flower garden like a coloured advertisement.' Almost exactly a century before, Sir Uvedale Price had written of 'Capability' Brown, whose style and system had dominated garden design since he worked at Warwick Castle in 1750: 'I have heard numberless instances of his arrogance and despotism, and such high pretensions seem to me little justified by his works.' And the attacks of Addison and Pope at the beginning of the century on our great formal gardens made by London and Wise in the grand geometrical manner of Le Nôtre will be familiar to every student of English literature.

In the art and fashion of garden design we are not only turncoats, but we go to the extent of obliterating what has gone before.

The great Victorian gardens which William Robinson derided have almost all disappeared. The structure of Barry's Shrubland remains practically entire; less exists of his Trentham Park; his terraces at Harewood and Cliveden remain. The style of formal, highly Victorian-style planting to which Robinson took such strong exception is still maintained at Drummond Castle in Perth. The design of the formal flower garden beside Westonbirt House laid out in 1844 remains very little changed. Here and there Victorian gardens are found, greatly simplified, and devoid of the ornate design and complex horticultural practices essential to the period.

Opposite: 'The Gardener'. Painting in oils by James Joseph Jacques Tissot, 1879. Formerly in the collection of Lt.-Colonel Leonard Messel.

The name of Barry is well remembered, though as an architect rather than a garden designer. Who today recalls the names, let alone know anything of the works of, William Sawrey Gilpin, who in the early years of Queen Victoria's reign is said to have had a monopoly in landscape gardening, or the immensely successful W. A. Nesfield (father of the much better-known architect W. E.) or Edward Milner? Paxton is known today as the designer of the Crystal Palace; yet he was an important garden architect, whom William Robinson thought had produced the 'greatest modern example of the waste of enormous means in making hideous a fine piece of ground'.

It is interesting to seek for the origins of the type of gardening which Robinson and his friends so despised. The landscape style with which Addison, Pope, Kent and the Earl of Burlington were so concerned, and which abolished avenues, geometrical parterres and regularity from our gardens—despatching the flowers into those great walled gardens discreetly hidden away so as not to be an 'unnatural' blot on the landscape—was apparently dominant when 'Capability' Brown, its most prolific exponent, died in 1783. It was carried on by his successor Humphry Repton, who died in 1818. By that time Uvedale Price had attacked the smoothness and dullness of these landscapes, urging the re-introduction of parterres and formality. He was, so far as I know, the first to urge on aesthetic and picturesque grounds the naturalising of plants and shrubs—for example kalmias, rhododendrons, azaleas and exotic trees—in our woodland walks.

Even more interesting is his enthusiasm for many of the views of the Rev. William Mason, as expressed in *The English Garden* of 1783. Mason was celebrated as a defender and apparent enthusiast for Brown; but Price was astute and subtle enough to see that this poem (particularly in the fourth book) was 'as real an attack on Mr Brown's system' as what he had written. We have only to look at Paul Sandby's pictures of the flower garden at Nuneham Park, so far as is known the only one that Mason himself designed, to realise that here was something created in the 1770's quite alien to the outlook of Brown and Repton: it had an astonishing similarity to the gardens of the early Victorian era which one sees illustrated. It was as full of trees, shrubs, and flowers in rich variety as it was in sentimental and romantic associations:

> On they past
> Thro' a wild thicket, till the perfum'd air
> Gave to another sense its prelude rich
> On what the eye should feast. But now the grove
> Expands; and now the Rose, the garden's Queen,
> Amidst her blooming subjects' humbler charms,
> On ev'ry plot her crimson pomp displays.
> 'Oh Paradise!' the ent'ring youth exclaim'd,
> 'Groves whose rich trees weep odorous gums and balm,
> 'Others whose fruit, burnish'd with golden rind,
> 'Hang aimiable, Hesperian fables true,
> 'If true, here only.'

This is, so to speak, the thought and poetry underlying the Nuneham garden. And how different from that 'smooth, simple path', with 'undulating line', of the Brownian style which Mason celebrates elsewhere!

The importance of this new conception of gardening in the late eighteenth century was that the views of Price were keenly supported by J. C. Loudon, the horticultural encyclopaedist and arboricultural expert and a writer of great authority who lived on into Victoria's reign. Another supporter was W. S. Gilpin, a considerable practitioner, whom I have already mentioned, and who lived until 1834. Sir Walter Scott was another influential disciple.

Therefore, when Queen Victoria came to the throne the scene was set for romantic and picturesque design and variety in planting, the return of architecture into gardening, with such features as garden houses, parterres, fountains, vases and other ornaments. In the greatly increased number of illustrated works published on the arts, every kind of style was advocated. Eclecticism was soon rampant.

There were other new and very significant factors in garden fashions. In 1838 Loudon had published his *Suburban Gardener and Villa Companion*. The growth of industry had produced a new class. No longer did those who had made money live near or even at their factories. They were moving into the new suburbs, away from the dark, Satanic mills, and to something to which they had been unused—a house with a garden. Loudon graded these people from fourth to first rate. The first-rate must have a park of between fifty and a hundred acres, and must surely have made a lot of money. For the wives of these Mrs Loudon, after her husband's death, published in 1845 *The Lady's Country Companion or How to Enjoy a Country Life Rationally*. The lady who has been so instructed enjoys a garden 'so brilliant with bright scarlet ver-

The garden front of Cheshunt Cottage, the residence of Wm. Harrison Esq., which had 'all that can render a country seat delightful'.

benas and gold yellow calceolarias, that you can scarcely gaze at it in the sunshine'.

The garden itself, quite apart from following in an increasingly less disciplined style the tenets of Price, was also changing rapidly with the remarkable developments in the practice of horti-culture. Greenhouses had in the first thirty years of the century changed out of all recognition, both in their structures and method of heating. Earlier they had been heated by smoke flues from fires, needing continuous attention, or by high-pressure steam blown through pipes. In the late 1820's it was generally realised that the circulation in pipes of water heated by a boiler was the simplest and most reliable method. In 1840 the great palm house at Kew was completed. It remains the most magnificent and indeed the most beautiful glass structure in England. In 1860 'hothouses for the million' built from standardised parts were being advertised.

None of these facts are mentioned in the writings of authorities on the picturesque and the romantic. Price, however, by his reference to and enthusiasm for the use of exotic plants, showed he was well aware of one change that was taking place, the introduction of fresh species from abroad.

In 1824 David Douglas set out for the Pacific coast of North America, which botanically and horticulturally had been little more than reconnoitred. Between then and his early death in 1832 the trees, shrubs and plants that he collected came into general cultivation. During Victoria's reign they altered not only the appearance of British gardens but subsequently of the landscape as well. Sensing that great things were on the way, a number of enthusiasts had developed arboreta and pineta. Lord Grenville began his collection at Dropmore in 1796, Robert Holford at Westonbirt in 1829, while the pinetum at Nuneham was started in 1834. Some of Douglas's original trees can still be identified in these and other old collections.

Douglas himself introduced the fir that bears his name, which far exceeds in height any native trees of Britain. He was followed by William Lobb, who collected from 1840 to 1857 and whose first trophy was the Chilean monkey-puzzle. A very few had been available before at £5 a plant. Lobb collected large quantities of seed for the firm of Veitch who in 1843 were able to advertise seedlings at 30s. a dozen: today no tree is more closely associated with Victoriana. In 1853 he introduced from California the wellingtonia, the biggest tree in the world. It soon became a status symbol, whose tall spire indicated from afar that here was a peer's or country gentleman's estate. At that time, too, the Scottish arboriculturists, not to be outdone, formed their own Oregon Association for whom John Jeffrey collected.

And conifers came from many other countries. The graceful Himalayan deodar with its pendulous branches—another eminent Victorian—after rather ineffectual introductions was raised here in thousands from 1841 onwards. A year or two later Lord Somers brought the Atlas cedar—bursting with superior Victorian energy and fecundity when compared with the long cultivated Lebanon—to his Victorian castle at Eastnor in Herefordshire (where the originals and numerous offspring may still be seen).

Finally, in 1860 John Gould Veitch brought from Japan another batch of newcomers which were soon established in every garden. Two rather small trees, called by the Japanese Hinoki and Sawara cypress and by the Victorians retinosporas, were planted in great numbers, being particularly favoured for cemeteries.

The Victorian enthusiasm for these conifers was almost uncontrolled, as was shown by their frequent misuse in places where their majesty (or in the case of the monkey-puzzle, curious geometry) could never adequately be appreciated. It was undoubtedly the Victorians' greatest and longest-lasting contribution not only to the landscape garden but to the smaller country house and suburban garden.

If one wishes to demonstrate this, take the famous walk round the lake at Stourhead. Remove (mentally!) all the conifers now growing there (many among the largest in the country and of dominating height) which were not even known to exist in the days of Henry Hoare, the creator of this great landscape. The general effect would be obviously startling even to the unknowledgeable.

With shrubs and herbaceous plants the effect was much less obvious. Gardens in Britain had long been full of flowers, while evergreen trees, and particularly conifers, were rarities. Yet the range of garden plants which the Victorians grew increased at an even greater rate than that of their trees. Douglas, for example, introduced *Mahonia aquifolium* in 1823. It is now naturalised, but for several years it fetched ten guineas a plant. The flowering red currant, the scented musk, *Nemophila insignis*, *Garrya elliptica*, the snowberry (*Symphoricarpus*), now naturalised in woods for the benefit of pheasants, clarkia and limnanthes—all were still choice plants when Victoria came to the throne. She had been queen for several years when the great flow of Chinese introductions began—to continue without break until the bamboo curtain clattered down only a few years ago. The London Horticultural Society sent Robert Fortune to Hong Kong in 1843. For the first time what we should now call technology entered into his collecting operations. Dr Nathaniel Bagshaw Ward, practising

The classical manner in Victorian form embellished with bedding-out

in the East End of London near the docks, accidentally found that he could keep plants alive for a long time in the desiccated air of a room by growing them in almost air-tight glass cases. From this invention was developed that most Victorian of drawing-room ornaments, the Wardian case, in which it was possible to grow the filmiest of ferns from humid, shady rocksides in the arid air of a gas-lit interior. This invention enabled Fortune to send living plants from the Orient on the long sea voyage through changing temperatures and climates to London.

Fortune made several journeys, the last of which included Japan. He ceased his travels in 1862. By then he had brought into cultivation, first as rarities but soon as everyman's plants, famous Victorian shrubs such as the winter-flowering jasmine (*Jasminum nudiflorum*), weigela (or diervilla), the Dutchman's breeches

A view in a 'select suburban residence illustrating the principles and practice of landscape gardening': Mount Grove, Hampstead, the seat of T. N. Longman, Esq. (1839).

(*Dicentra spectabilis*), forsythia, *Prunus triloba*, *Primula japonica*, some of the first Asiatic rhododendrons and azaleas, florist's tree paeonies, collections of the first pom-pom chrysanthemums from China, and later a collection of Japanese chrysanthemums.

The other great event of Victoria's reign was undoubtedly the beginning of rhododendronomania. This is a limited activity, as it can only be practised on certain (acid) soils and only be fully extended in our milder counties. Joseph Dalton Hooker (later knighted) was in India between 1847 and 1851. He collected a great variety of Himalayan rhododendrons, an account of whose magnificence was displayed in the plates of his *Rhododendrons of Sikkim-Himalaya* (1849), and whose seeds he distributed widely, particularly in Cornwall. This resulted not only in these shrubs being naturalised but in their blood flowing in hundreds of hybrids.

Finally there developed another mania, also limited, but this time by financial considerations, that of the orchid. The inadequacy of greenhouses had made their cultivation difficult. The first English firm to grow them commercially was probably Loddiges of Hackney, who issued the first catalogue of their collection in 1839. By 1856 the first of the countless hybrids that are still being raised today was produced.

The camellia had a boom in the early days of the reign. Then a visit to the nursery of Chandler and Son to see the new kinds was a social occasion—though when the son in the partnership died in 1896 the flower had, to his grief, gone out of favour.

But pre-eminent in the Victorian garden was 'bedding out'. It does not seem to have become fashionable until the late 1850's, when, in a book on the use of beautiful-leaved plants, the popular writer Shirley Hibberd referred to the practice in recent years 'adopted freely in his masterly system of embellishing the parterre with sub-tropical plants at Battersea Park'.

The other great feature of the Victorian garden was the introduction of mechanisation. Like much else we have mentioned, this began just before the magic year of 1837, but it did not become widely known until 'Mr Budding's machine for cropping or shearing the vegetable surface of lawns, grass plots, etc.' was introduced. This machine was identical in principle with almost all subsequent mowing machines. It introduced the cult of the lawn. Formerly grass plots were scythed, and the short, regularly clipped sward that the new mower produced was unknown. As the makers claimed, 'the eye will never be offended by those circular scars, inequalities, and bare places so commonly made by the best mowers with the scythe and which continue visible for several days'. The machine was immensely successful. Soon improved models were introduced by rival manufacturers—such as the first one to throw the grass into a hood and so avoid

An Elizabethan Pavilion of 1866 by John Arthur Hughes

the need for raking it up. The machine made easy work of cutting round the flower beds scattered all over the lawn in a variety of shapes and in parterre-like patterns. Grass, indeed, now replaced the coloured gravels, spars, pit coal, brick dust and yellow sands on which the patterns of London and Wise were worked. The very English cult of the lawn, which today has become an obsession, can therefore be claimed as of early Victorian origin.

Many other commonplaces of garden practice originated at this time. For instance, on March 4, 1839, 'S.T.' of Stoke Ferry, Norfolk, wrote to the *Gardener's Magazine* pointing out that the recently introduced wire netting used for penning sheep was ideal for protecting gardens against rabbits and hares. And it should be mentioned that gardening was becoming an appropriate pursuit for women: in 1840 came Mrs Loudon's *Gardening for Ladies*. There were great changes, too, in fruit growing. Apples, pears, grapes, peaches, pineapples—the cultivation and breeding of these were transformed by the remarkable work of Thomas Andrew Knight, from 1811 to his death in 1838 President of the then Horticultural Society of London.

This Society, founded in 1807, was honoured with the prefix 'Royal' (the 'London' being omitted) in 1861. In that year their new gardens at Kensington were opened by the Prince Consort. He described them 'as an attempt at least to reunite the science of art and gardening to the sister arts of architecture, sculpture and painting'. The architecture was in the hands of Fowke and Smirke, the gardening in the hands of W. A. Nesfield—soldier turned painter turned garden designer. The style could be described as high Victorian, of the kind that William Robinson and Miss Jekyll abhorred. The most prominent feature was four flower-less beds outlined in box, representing the rose, thistle, shamrock and leek. These were worked out in white Derbyshire spar; purple blue john or fleur spar; pale blue Welsh slate; red, pounded red brick; yellow, pounded yellow brick. Also used were fragments of coloured glass. Elsewhere, these materials were used to line flower-beds to give colour when the beds were empty of plants in winter and to blend with them in summer when within them grew scarlet pelargonium, violet verbena, orange tropaeolum, silver-leaved pelargonium, calceolarias and lobelia. Artificial stone was used—and was by now general—for fountains, urns, vases and statuary of all periods and styles, mingled according to taste.

Nesfield, latterly assisted by his son Markham, worked in this style far into Victoria's reign. It was said of him with every justification that he approached gardening not as one loving nature. Most of his work has disappeared, but examples or remaining fragments of it exist at Witley Court in Worcestershire (with his great fountain, in its time the biggest and best in England); Kinmel in North Wales; Drayton in Northamptonshire; and Castle Howard, Broughton Hall and Grimston in Yorkshire. With Sir W. J. Hooker he planned the arboretum at Kew Gardens and also some formal work which was long ago tactfully removed.

So far we have discussed the gardens that Loudon put in his higher classes. Yet we should not forget that most of the new gardens of Victoria's reign were in or not much above the fourth class—up to one acre. And it was to this class, with little country or horticultural background, that much literature, modifying the grand manner, was addressed. 'Good taste' was the watchword. It was demonstrated in the small conservatory, the window decorations displaying into the street, the crude rockeries, and the fern cases. And, unable to afford masonry for the garden buildings, rustic-work became universal, either to span, say, a ditch, or almost invariably in every garden to provide an arbour or summer house—the more ornate, the more socially acceptable.

Not the least important feature of the late Victorian age was the development of hybrids, with the aim of producing more violently coloured flowers. The developments towards this end were extremely successful in spite of the fact that Mendel's laws were still unknown and the science of genetics as yet not invented. And there is abundant evidence to show that Victorian gardeners—florists and vegetable- and fruit-growers—produced results of the highest quality as good as if not better than we can achieve today. They were without the innumerable chemicals that we automatically use today. But they had horses. And plenty of labour, much of which had learned the hard way. And, to give them their due, even the engravings illustrating Victorian gardening periodicals, and many of the lovely coloured lithographs they included, have seldom been excelled by the camera.

These were the features of the Victorian era that have passed away. The legacy that is left is surely the large number of plants that are true Victorians, having been introduced during the great Queen's reign, which are still found in every garden today.

'A suitable style of summer house for the average large garden', 1895

Thoughts on Bridges

WOOD-ENGRAVINGS AND
REFLECTIONS
BY GEORGE MACKLEY

CROSSING our bridges when we come to them, we see some that are purely utilitarian devices. They may move us physically, but they leave us spiritually unmoved. There are structures based on intellect, coupled with a restrained and austere aestheticism. We may see others that are the work of patient and devoted handcraftsmen, guided by an inspired creative designer. And occasionally we find one which is enhanced by a crowning work of piety.

The river and the bridge meet where their paths cross. The men who built a bridge often built a community, and created a focal point for those who use it, who have a feeling for its historical past and who desire to maintain its dignity.

CATARACT

IN OPEN PLACES among small stones and shallow watercourses the little streams play unselfconsciously, but as they move onward a strange bashfulness becomes apparent and they seek seclusion among leafy depths and rocky places to disport themselves in privacy. As they become more staid in maturity they may adopt a more dignified course, though this may lead them to a far from benign approach to a cataract with a snarl of anger and foaming fury.

Some dwelling houses by the bridge have turned their backs on the violence of the river. Only one or two of these stand near its brink.

The cataract demands its own way. On occasion it smiles on those who approach it, though a fringe of far-flung stones, torn-up trees and water-worn boulders show what it can do to those whom it resents.

COTSWOLD BRIDGE

ONE WHO insulates or isolates himself in a moving car may achieve a degree of immunity, but he who is captivated by the intimacies of the brooks, flowers and waving grasses is responding as many generations have done before him. There is nothing like a running stream to create this response and to induce a state of prolonged contemplation. How many must have decided that one of the greatest needs of humanity is a pair of reinforced elbows, enabling them to lean for hours on the parapet, enjoying the pattern of the lichen-covered stones, the strands of ivy, the cool ferns shaded by the bridge, the gently waving weeds and the playing fishes beyond. Those who have a solemn nature may well brood on the old stonework of the house and mill where many may have dwelt and worked, among the great dark trees that give depth to their memories.

FOOTBRIDGES

Those who approach the river bank find themselves confronted by a pattern of white wooden bridges, each with a clean curving line of water in front of it and the tumultuous roar of a tumbling bay behind it. On the margin of this smooth surface which descends into the depths one sees a fringe of quivering water weeds. Below the swirl of dark, menacing waters one sees a tangle of water-washed willow roots, while, at a distance, where the waters are gently subsiding, the weeds are barely moving beside the flowery banks beyond.

Whether one leans on one railing to meditate beside the placid water of the river on one side or leans on the other railing to contemplate the furies below him, one is as likely as not to be called back to reality by the imperious ringing of a bicycle bell demanding the idler to make way.

THE LITTLE BRIDGE

ALL STREAMS begin somewhere. Some creep out of dark places between stones, some bubble out from crystal-clear springs, while some emerge from reedy and flowery places from which their precise origin cannot be determined. Many have no status; but the presence of an old bridge, a stone bastion on a rocky bed, make it clear that they possess latent powers which wise men have learnt not to ignore.

CHURCH PATH

IN THE VILLAGE are lanes and footpaths where there stand groups of cottages across which can be seen the soft green verges of slowly moving brooks. Here and there the lanes are linked by footways running from one shady green to another, each crossed by a narrow plank bridge known as a 'bro'. One much favoured is the 'bro' where the path is lost to view beyond the lych gate, the church and the dark shades of the trees.

TREES BY A BRIDGE

THE BROAD river pauses by a lock which saw long service when the needs of the towns and villages depended upon the boatmen, and the needs of the boatmen depended upon the services of the inn lurking behind the willows. The mill stream leads to some small wooden bridges, each with its footpath, its tumbling bay and its group of venerable trees. Beyond these, out of sight, but within sound of yet another sluice, stands what is left of the great mill, which once turned two wheels. In times of flood it can make its voice heard and its presence felt when the gates are opened and the great eddies sweep on their way.

Hidden by the trees is the church, which, like others in the placid water meadows, proclaims by the loftiness of its spire its religious and architectural aspirations.

MIJNDENSESLUIS

AMAZE of streams enter or leave one another until in the
distance they lose themselves in further complexities.
They pass castles, the raised arms of white lift bridges,
gabled houses with colourful waterside gardens, while here and
there can be seen the dignified mansion of a merchant with its
copper beech, trim lawns and gazebo. One approaches Mijnden-
sesluis along winding, tree-lined roads beside farmhouses and
thatched hay barns to the place where the lift bridge stands. At
leisure along comes the man to operate the 'Ophaal Brug'
giving access to the lock beyond. Here the boats sail through the
many lakes left by the old peat workings.

The sound of the boats having died away, the bridge with its
rattling chain has once more been lowered, tranquillity has been
restored and the passers-by resume their leisurely course.

BOERDERIJ

THE WATER hardly moves between and beyond the dark trees; the cows move over the little bridge quietly from pasture to pasture; a hen may cackle; and there may be the clank of a pail or the clatter of wooden 'klompen'. Here the old man was born and here he hopes to spend his remaining days.

One who seeks to depict the textures of timber, thatch and mellow brick will find all that he asks, much as Rembrandt found them in his day and age. If he turns his back he will find more than he expected. Above him rises the mass of a great technological university, which has bought the old man's land, offers him a home as long as he needs it, invites him to tend the vast collection of house plants which no Dutch institution can do without, and leaves him to milk his cows in peace.

FENLAND RIVER

FENLAND RIVERS call sometimes for broad aspects and
sometimes for intimate detail, such as patches of arrow-
head, sedge and reed, over which are seen reflections of
cows, wooden fences and groups of willows. At remoter dis-
tances are geometrical patterns of ditches, yellow corn crops,
framed always by the eternal sedge, endeavouring to restore it
to the rustle of the breeze and the song of the birds that knew it
so long. The great flatness is relieved by low hills, a massive
church, a fine cluster of farm buildings or a manor house. Not
all venerable farmsteads possess beauty or elegance, but changing light can do so much for them.

To recall us to the river and its willows we have a word with
one of the fen men as he opens the locks which he calls 'doors',
and he lets in a swirl of water to cover the mossy darkness below.

MOUNTAIN STREAM

FROM the remote fastnesses and from the forbidding chasms
the mountain streams plunge with mighty force on their
powerful way. Sometimes the waters broaden into a reed-
fringed lake, pausing while they are joined by gentler trickles
from marshes before they together resume, lower down, their
headlong furious fight against boulders and shattered trees.

Within the confines of the valleys between the high hills some
people must perforce dwell, close to the rushing of its powerful
waters. Some appear to prefer to build their habitations with
their front doors on the more tranquil side of the street, though
some more hardy are not averse to living near its spray and roar.

As the stream moves on it slowly forsakes its vehement
passion and assumes a mellow urbanity, allowing wild irises to
bloom in its quiet waters and permitting even a small house to
consort with it.